The Envelope: Walking up to Everest Base Camp

The Envelope

Walking up to Everest Base Camp

by

ANDREW STEVENSON

Vajra Publications
www.vajrabooks.com.np

Published by

Vajra Publications

Jyatha, Thamel, P.O. Box 21779, Kathmandu, Nepal
Tel.: 977-1-4220562, Fax: 977-1-4246536
e-mail: bidur_la@mos.com.np
www.vajrabooks.com.np

Distributor

Vajra Book Shop

Kathmandu, Nepal

ISBN 978-9937-506-27-4

Printed in Nepal

For
Katie and Cooper

Table of Contents

1

Kathmandu

A hastily scrawled note in my key-box at the Kathmandu Guest House:

We're in the New Orleans Café. Come meet us.

Jamie.

Jamie?

It's almost ten at night. Despite the curfew, I leave the Kathmandu Guest House, walk twenty metres and turn down a dark alleyway to the New Orleans Café. Several stray dogs lie curled together for warmth between heaps of rubbish. At 1,600 metres, the air is damp and biting cold.

Incense wafts on the air, blocking out the rancid smells from the street. The place is quieter than usual. Locals, from among the Nepalese elite who can afford to while away their hours in cafes like this, mingle with Western climbers and trekkers. I recognize Jamie McGuinness sitting with his girlfriend Suzanne at a table beside a flaming brazier. I last saw them two years ago, in the village of Tal, on the Annapurna Circuit; Jamie was returning with a group of friends from one of the trekking peaks. The writer of a guidebook on the Everest region, Jamie is a well-known figure in climbing circles.

"How'd you know I was here?" I drag a chair over to join them.

"Saw the posters advertising your Annapurna slide shows." Although a Kiwi, Jamie's accent is as indefinable as mine. We are probably equally rootless, although I call Bermuda home now. "What are you doing?" he asks.

"The Annapurna Circuit," I reply, sitting down slowly.

"Again?"

I nod.

Having written the Trailblazer guidebook on trekking in the Everest region, Jamie is probably as favourably biased on the Solo Khumbu as I am on the Annapurnas. While I haven't written a guidebook on the Annapurnas, my Annapurna narrative and photographic book are still in print. "Ever been to Everest?" he asks.

I shake my head.

"Try it, instead of doing the same treks all the time," he says, signalling a waiter and then pulling out a pen and a sheet of paper. The waiter takes my order of a beer. "How many days have you got?"

"Twenty days trekking, leaving enough time in Kathmandu to make sure I get my flight out."

"OK. Start at Jiri." Jamie automatically slips into his role of guide as he lists the villages I should stay at. "Jiri. Deorali. Sete. Junbesi. That's a really beautiful village. Nuntala/Manidingma. Bubsa. Chaplung or Phakding and up to Namche Bazaar, by-passing Lukla. Then Khunde, Tengboche, Pangboche, Dingboche, Duglha, Lobuche, Gorak Shep and Kala Pattar, the hill overlooking Everest Base Camp. Then cross over the Cho La pass to Tragnag and then Gokyo. After climbing Gokyo Ri, down to Dole, Namche Bazaar and then Lukla." He adds the total number of days. "Twenty days. You can do it."

I haven't even the vaguest idea of the route, the places, what I might see. For someone who has travelled over most of Nepal, I'm remarkably ignorant about Everest and the Solo Khumbu; all I know is gleaned from reading about climbing expeditions to the summit of the tallest mountain in the world. Jamie's detailed itinerary isn't enough to persuade me.

"I was going to leave tomorrow for the Annapurnas," I tell him.

"The Maoists are calling a bus strike tomorrow," Jamie reminds me, shaking his head. "You'll never get to the trailhead unless you walk all the way from Kathmandu. But if the bus drivers are still striking, you could fly to Lukla and walk up to Everest instead. The pilots aren't on strike."

A Maoist general strike preventing me from leaving as planned for the Annapurnas and the chance meeting with Jamie tonight is like preordained fate. I believe in these things, the twists and turns of circumstance that shape one's life. Tired, still a little jet lagged, and pooped after giving the slide show and answering questions, I am not in the most enterprising of moods.

"What are you doing in the morning?" Jamie asks, sensing my frame of mind.

"Nothing. Not if there's a strike."

"I've a breakfast meeting here. We can go over this again after my meeting. I'll show you some wild passes to cross and cool alternative routes." He studies me intently, emphasizing the point. I notice the pupil of his left eye is enlarged and mention this to him. He looks to Suzanne for sympathy. "Must be damage to the retina after climbing Cho Oyu earlier this year," he tells us.

"What's Cho Oyu?" I ask.

"Eight thousand two hundred metre mountain, the sixth highest in the world," Jamie tells me as a preamble to describing the climb. My eyes glaze over with fatigue. It's hard to identify with his enthusiasm; I can't imagine climbing a mountain so high.

"You going to be here too?" I ask Suzanne. She was a Peace Corps volunteer in the Khumbu area for a couple of years and has just come back to Kathmandu after trekking there for the last couple of weeks. I'd like her opinion.

"I'll be here, writing," she replies.

"Writing what?"

"Master's thesis on the ecological effects of tourism on the Khumbu and the Sherpa people."

"Maybe while we're waiting for Jamie to finish his meeting you can tell me what you think." I trust her objectivity and her viewpoint more than Jamie's esoteric climber's enthusiasm. Suzanne's spent time staying with the local people, following the common hiking trails used by more plebeian trekkers like me, not bagging summits or crossing wild passes.

I look at my watch. I can barely keep my eyes open. Stiff from sitting down for an hour, I get up from the table. I feel like a ninety-year old man.

Suzanne asks, "What's wrong?"

"My back." I lean on the chair for support, hoping to relieve the pain. "I had an accident five months ago."

"Can you handle trekking?" she asks, as I try to stand upright.

"Sure."

I'm not sure at all but I'm not admitting that now. The last time I saw Jamie and Suzanne, I was using my old one hundred-litre pack, and carrying thirty kilos.

"You can't carry your own pack," Suzanne insists.

"I'll take a porter."

We say goodnight and they head off to Jamie's apartment. I return to my room at the iconic Kathmandu Guest House, a converted old Rana palace and the epicentre of tourism development in Thamel. I slip under the covers and turn off the light and then toss and turn on the bed. The floor of the Guest House cinema above my room thumps with a pirated DVD copy of The English Patient.

I've had my mind set on doing the Annapurna Circuit again, for how long? I calculate the time: exactly five months and fifteen days. But no one knows the reason why I am here. In the darkness of the hotel room, I fumble for the sealed envelope lying on the bedside table.

⁓

Bleary-eyed and still jet-lagged, I meet Suzanne at the New Orleans Café. She is having breakfast. Jamie is deep in discussion a couple of tables away. Suzanne wears a tightly fitting blouse over her square shoulders and a cloth skirt wrapped around her flat stomach, which discretely envelops her long legs. With her flowing blonde hair, blue eyes and angular but soft facial features, she's the male mountaineer's fantasy of a girlfriend. Strong enough to carry a heavy pack and be a valuable member of a climbing team she's also exquisitely feminine. It's her eyes that are the most alluring, but there's a hint of sadness to them too.

"I just remembered," Suzanne says, as I order a small pot of milk coffee and an omelette. "You have trouble with altitude don't you?"

"At around two thousand eight hundred metres, I start getting an altitude headache," I tell her, surprised that she can remember my propensity for altitude sickness. "Why?"

"Maybe you should try to spend more time at the higher elevations to acclimatize better for Everest Base Camp and Gokyo."

"Meaning?" I ask.

"Even if there is no bus strike, don't walk from Jiri, fly in to Lukla. If you walk from Jiri, you cross the grain of mountain ranges," Suzanne says, "so it's a lot of ups and downs over the foothills with some passes perhaps as high as Lukla. Great for getting into shape, but you're fit already and you've experienced the Nepalese foothills, so your time might be better spent getting into the higher elevations of the Khumbu straight away, acclimatizing to higher altitudes where you know you have problems. Be a shame though to cut out the stretch from Jiri to Phakding because it is the most unspoiled part of the Everest trek. Seems everyone flies in to Lukla now and just walks up from there."

As she talks, I try and imagine the places she describes, the foothills and ranges, the Sherpa villages.

"I know the Khumbu's got great views and everything," I say, "but is it a nice area to trek in? The spiritual aspects, I mean." For me, it's not just a question of conquering high altitude passes and mountains. But I don't explain to Suzanne my real motive in asking these more metaphorical questions. And she doesn't ask.

"It's beautiful in a desolate way, and stark, but the Sherpa people make up for that." She sees my hesitation. "It's different from the Annapurnas," she says. "Like comparing apples with oranges."

Jamie suddenly appears with a friend of his, another lean, craggy-faced climber.

"We're going over to Pilgrims Bookstore to look at some maps," he tells Suzanne. "I'll be back in a few minutes."

They leave. Suzanne raises her cup of tea to her mouth with both hands. I remember those capable hands from our first encounter on the Annapurna Circuit; masculine in size and strength, there is nevertheless a feminine elegance about them too.

I order another pot of coffee.

"You're having real troubles making up your mind about this aren't you?" Her voice is low now, and private. She understands, or suspects, more than I realize. I nod. I haven't told her everything. In fact, I have not told her anything. She watches me closely.

"At your slide shows about the Annapurnas you push people to do what they think they can't do," she says. "You get others to do the twenty-one day circuit of the Annapurnas but now you're not stretching yourself to head up to Everest. Why's it such a big decision?"

I like Suzanne. I liked her when I met her two years ago. She's quiet, but honest and straightforward. And she exudes an inner quality that makes me inclined to trust and confide in her.

"There's a favourite spot of mine in the Annapurnas," I tell her, "on the high route between Upper Pisang and Braga. It's an ethereal, spiritual place." She smiles and listens. I don't have to spell out to her where this marvellous stretch is on the north side of the Himalayas, she's been there. She knows you can see up and down the valley, from Tilicho Lake all the way down to Paungda Danda. I've spent hours sitting there watching the alpine choughs playing in the wind. On the opposite side of the valley are the Annapurnas. Everywhere there are *mani* walls, prayer flags, *kanis*, prayer stones, *chortens, and gompas.* "I always thought that when I die I'd like my ashes to be thrown out to the winds up there." Unexpectedly, I feel a surge of emotions surging within me. I can no longer finish the words I wanted to say.

She waits.

There is a long silence before I explain, "My brother died seven months ago." I mumble, my voice small, the words barely audible. I've never had to explain his death to anyone. Everyone back home in Bermuda, where most of my family finally settled, knew my brother. I wipe tears away with the back of my hand. "At the funeral home, he was lying in an open casket. I cut some of his hair. I have it here, in an envelope." I touch my shirt pocket. "I want to burn the envelope, where I imagined my own ashes being thrown to the winds one day."

I can't think about Kevin's death, let alone talk about it, without my feelings surfacing raw and tender. I look up to see Suzanne's eyes are also brimming with tears.

"Six weeks after my brother died in April, I had an accident on my motorbike."

"Oh God. How bad?"

"It was very bad. I shattered a vertebra into fragments," I answer. I have only told a couple of people what I'm about to tell Suzanne. "I lost consciousness. When I came to, in the middle of the road, I couldn't move my legs. I was scared I'd be paralysed." I feel a shiver down my back. It is almost December and even in Kathmandu it is already cold and damp. In the centre of the restaurant, glowing logs burn in an open steel barrel. "Lying there in intense pain, I had this intense feeling that my brother was near. He wasn't in this world any more, but he wasn't entirely gone either. He was like, in between, floating, looking down at me. The expression on his face told me that this shouldn't happen, that our family had had to endure enough with his death." I press a forefinger and thumb against my eyelids to squeeze out the tears. "Fire trucks came, and then the ambulance. They straightened my legs to strap me onto a board to immobilise my spine. I've never felt pain like that before." I stop. It's impossible to explain to anyone how profound the fear is when you think you may never walk again.

"Everything is okay now?" Suzanne asks, quietly.

I nod. But it didn't look good back then. X-rays and then a CAT-Scan revealed the extent of the damage. Annabel, my girlfriend, an orthopaedic specialist, arrived at the hospital and told me the truth: it was worse than the doctors had originally thought. The vertebra had burst into fragments, crushed by the impact into a score of small pieces. A surgeon was called in but he was reluctant to operate because the vertebra was too unstable. A chunk had slipped into my spinal column. They immobilized me in two back braces. I was on morphine, a catheter, and a drip for the first five days. After running a marathon race the day before the accident, I spent two and a half months encased in two back braces, the first six weeks mostly on my back in bed, waiting for the damaged vertebra to fuse together. They let me out of hospital on condition that Annabel took responsibility for me. From grieving for my brother, I focussed on healing my body. Those first weeks out of the hospital were the most intense days of my life.

Barely five months later, I'm in Nepal, in a tiny restaurant, sitting across the table from Suzanne.

"I'm okay now," I assert, wiping away the wetness on my cheeks with the ball of my thumbs. "I made up my mind that I'd be healed enough to do this trip before the end of the trekking season."

This is what saved me. The dream of walking in the Himalayas again was my psychological lifeline. I visualized going back to that spot on the high route north of the Annapurnas, to burn the envelope with Kevin's hair. It would be my own symbolic way of coming to terms with his death. But it would also be a way of thanking him, not just for being my brother, but for somehow intervening that day of my accident. I can't explain it, but I believe Kevin was there, to lend a hand with my own fate.

Suzanne is quiet for some time.

"You're sure you'll manage the trip?" she asks.

"Yes."

In truth, Annabel wasn't even sure I'd be able to handle sitting almost upright during the long flight from Bermuda to London, then on to Kathmandu. It's been only two months since I was encased in back-braces and I am still incredibly stiff and sore. I'd only just started to drive my car.

Suzanne removes the cups and pots from the table. She takes the best map of the Khumbu Himal, one of the detailed topographical maps published in Germany, and spreads it out before us.

"There's a beautiful spot here, above the village of Khumjung, above the village *gompa*," she says, and marks it X. "It's very peaceful. I saw a sky burial there on my last trip."

I study the map and then look at her. My emotions are too raw and I want to change the subject.

"What about you? What are you doing now?" I ask, diverting from the sorrow that still afflicts me at a second's notice.

"Leaving in a couple of days for the States."

"Must be hard for you and Jamie to be so far away from each other."

"We're not going out together any more," she says, explaining the sadness I had seen in her eyes.

"I'm sorry." It's all I can think of saying.

"After years of going out with mountaineers, I've decided I'm going to climb mountains for my own sake," Suzanne says with quiet defiance. "I have three wonderful loving big-hearted brothers and when I think about it, I don't know many big-hearted climbers. They are all so egocentric."

As if on cue, Jamie returns and sits at the table with us.

"How was the meeting?" Suzanne asks.

"Ah, I dunno," Jamie says. He seems dejected. "If he'd really wanted me to join his team I would have, but it was more like, well, if *I* really want to join him, I can." He sees the Khumbu map and brightens as he tells me, "You could do some really wild routes around the Everest area." He passes his hands over the map, trying to persuade me to do things I know I'm not capable of. "Distances aren't that great. You could walk up this valley and cross over the pass. There are some staggering views."

He begins to name the spectacular views from the peaks of mountains, speaking with familiarity, as if they were street names in his local neighbourhood. The passes are all about six and a half thousand metres, higher than Mt. McKinley, the highest mountain in North America. They are a couple of thousand metres higher than Mt. Blanc, the highest mountain in Europe. Twice as high as Mt. Cook in New Zealand. And he's just talking about the passes, the low points between the mountain peaks.

Even if I hadn't broken my back, even if I could do these wild routes, I have not come here for the views. I find myself fumbling at my shirt pocket again, and quickly pull my hand away.

Meanwhile Jamie's hands sweep over the flattened map.

"You wouldn't have any problem doing this in a day," he says, as if my little feet could get me across the depicted mountains as easily. It's a relief when he pontificates on his own future climbing plans, which are not quite as modest or metaphysical as my own. He is organising a trans-Himalayan walk but must find a film crew first. His plans described, there is an awkward silence. Jamie looks at his watch. "Gotta go."

Suzanne and I get up as well.

"Have you decided what you're going to do?" she asks me.

I think for a second before I reply. The chance meeting with Jamie and Suzanne, the continuing bus strike delaying my start on the Annapurnas, it's as if it was meant to be.

"I'll fly to the Everest region," I say, giving up on the plans concocted while lying immobile on my back, and accepting the challenge of trekking in a new area. I've always been good at dropping imperatives, making last minute decisions, and redefining goals. Who knows, Everest may be more spiritually meaningful to me than the Annapurnas, and there's only one way to find out.

2

Flying to Lukla

The Twin Otter brushes over the mountain pass, skirting perilously close to a near-vertical mountainside before it banks left to fly up a rocky canyon. Enormous sacks of rice and sugar stacked like a ship's ballast, partially block the view down the aisle to the cockpit. We jostle in the turbulence as the pilot flies blindly into puffs of mist hanging off the towering cliffs. I swallow hard and hold my nose to equalize. My throat feels as if it is on fire. I've either caught a cold, or my throat has reacted to the pollution of Kathmandu. Or both. I can no longer be in Kathmandu more than a few days before the polluted air gives me a sore throat, runny eyes, and a headache.

We break out of the clouds. The vibration of the engine and hum of propellers change as the pilot adjusts the angle of the propeller blades to full pitch, and increases the RPM. We jolt forward against our seatbelts as the props bite into the air. The captain's fist clenches two adjacent throttle handles protruding from the top of the cockpit. The co-pilot, a woman, adjusts the friction control. Through the cockpit window, beyond the tangle of hands and forearms juggling the controls, appears a tiny patch of level ground on top of a spur in the steep-sided valley.

The nose dips as the flaps extend and we continue our final approach to the patch of flat ground perched on a ridge. There will be no second chance; our pilot has to put the aircraft down first time or not at all. Fall short and we crash into the valley. Float too long and we crash into a vertical rock face at the top end of the short runway. The altitude of the airstrip, I read in Jamie's guidebook, varies twenty metres, from top to bottom.

Crosswinds gusting down the valley blow the Twin Otter off course and the pilot applies more throttle as we power in, crab-like, over the threshold. Through the window I watch until the wheels float a tantalising few centimetres over the gravel before settling onto the rough ground in a burst of dust and scattered stones. The pilot reverses the propeller blades and opens the throttle again to brake our onward rush up the hillside. Gravity, disc brakes, and the reversed props slow us down before the rock wall at the end of the runway.

Lukla.

I peer out the side window as we pivot around a turning area carved out of the hillside. Trekkers' lodges are scattered in what were once potato fields. Hundreds of Nepalese and foreign trekkers squat on the embankment and watch the pilot manoeuvre. As the outside left wing pirouettes in a wide axis, the wingtip ploughs into the rock face, scraping off the navigation lights. People yell, pointing, before the pilot cuts the engines and steps outside the aircraft. Despite being a Nepalese, he's wearing a black leather aviator's jacket, Ray Ban aviator sunglasses, black leather driving gloves, and pointy cowboy boots. As he smokes a cigarette he calmly assesses the damaged wingtip.

Crawling over the sacks of food in the companionway, I disembark and walk stiffly over to witness the damage. A gaping hole has perforated the wingtip. The red port light hangs down by its wires. I suck in a lungful of cold, fresh mountain air and look around me as three aircraft, another Twin Otter, a long-nosed Dornier, and a Chinese Yak, hurtle down the runway, one after the other.

Waiting for my backpack to be unloaded from the nose of the aircraft, I watch an enterprising Nepalese patching the wingtip with strips of silver duct tape.

"You want porter? Guide?" A swarm of porters and guides accost me when they see me pick up my own backpack.

"I'm with a group," I tell them, magic words that fend them off without further argument. Groups have already arranged the hiring of their trekking guides and porters.

Despite the damage to its wing, the Twin Otter is filled again with baggage. Tents, folding chairs, iron dining tables, kerosene stoves along with the trekkers' packs, are shoved into the aircraft's fore and aft storage compartments until nothing else can be crammed in. Luggage compartment hatches are forcibly pressed shut. Trekkers climb into the cabin, less concerned with the plane's airworthiness than their desire to get the hell out of the mountains. When the few last strips of duct tape are stretched over the mangled wingtip, the local manager for the airline steps back to admire his improvised repair job and gives the pilot a thumbs up.

Undeterred by his previous lack of judgement, the pilot taxis to the starting point of the runway where the aircraft perches at an angle, nose down. He gives full throttle, releases the wheel brakes and the aircraft lunges forward, downhill, rushing towards the gaping chasm. It's no longer an aircraft taking off a runway so much as an overloaded piece of machinery on wheels hurtling down a ski-jump. The heavily loaded Twin Otter sags reluctantly off the ground at the end of the airstrip and slumps into the yawning gap below before reappearing far down the valley.

The duct tape worked.

A moment later another Twin Otter lands. The same familiar high-pitched sound as the plane charges up the airstrip and the throttles are applied with the propeller blades reversed to slow the aircraft down. The venerable Twin Otter turns at the end of the runway revealing, to my astonishment, silver duct-tape covering a damaged wingtip probably incurred in a similar accident on the same hillside.

Carrying my heavy pack on my back and another daypack on my front, I stagger into the dining room of a lodge. Fifteen Westerners sitting on Tibetan carpets laid out on bench seats in front of trunk-sized tables watch me. I unload my packs and despite the sign on the kitchen warning, *STAFF ONLY*, I enter the kitchen to ask for *dal bhaat*. The proprietor scowls at me and makes it plain that I am not welcome in the kitchen. Meekly, I return to the dining room and sit down with the others.

"Travelling on yer own are yer?" The question comes from a bearded man with a very distinct Australian accent.

"Yeah. You?" I reply.

"With a group." The Beard indicates the others sitting around. "Just arrived. Heading up to Tengboche with my wife." They are as excited as I am at the prospect of hiking into the mountains. "Name's Bruce."

Mixing with the Australians, I eat rice, lentils and curried potatoes. But I have little appetite, blowing my nose as often as putting food into my mouth. Soon the table is littered with blobs of tissue crumpled around greenish-yellow globs.

Bruce the Beard's group have stopped for lunch at the lodge before heading out. I am short of breath and the slightest effort takes all my energy. With a full-blown cold coming on, and classic symptoms of altitude sickness, I decide to spend the night in Lukla. I drag my pack into a simple room partitioned with thick, roughly hewn slabs of wood. To kill time, I write postcards in the warmth of the dining room and then wander over to the post office, savouring the exoticism of being thrust so easily into the foothills of the Himalayas. The ramshackle wooden building serving as the district post office hardly looks like an official government building. The Nepalese man sitting at a wooden desk studiously ignores me although there is no one else in the room. He stares glassy-eyed at an open ledger book. After a couple of minutes, he says, "Yes," without looking up.

"*Namaste*. I'd like to buy some stamps, please."

He doesn't reply, and he doesn't move. He stares at the ledger, making me wait. I stand there patiently. Finally he asks, "How many?"

"Six post cards."

He looks at me, then opens a wooden box, and searches under a layer of papers. He pulls out two used stamps and extracts a messy bottle of glue from a drawer in the desk. I watch as he glues the back of the second-hand stamps before carefully placing it on the corner of the postcards.

"Are these new stamps?" I ask. They patently are used ones but that doesn't stop me from asking. He doesn't answer but he does pull open another drawer and removes a book with sheets of new stamps interlaced in its pages. He separates four new stamps and licks their backs before placing them on the postcards. He places the stamps on each postcard with meticulous detail so that each stamp extends over the postcard's edge. This will make it easier to pull the stamp off the postcard again. He calculates the total on a piece of paper.

I take the cards and stamps and let him keep the change.

"Wait." He reaches a hand out for the cards. "I send Kathmandu."

I ignore the outstretched hand and quickly pocket the postcards. I will find someone later to mail them from Kathmandu.

Outside the post office again, I look to the south, where bruised purple clouds haemorrhage in the lower end of valley. The aircraft ferrying passengers in and out of Lukla have stopped their shuttle service. The atmosphere has grown quieter now that the porters seeking employment have disappeared. When I return to the dining room at the lodge, I make my way to a space heater in the centre of the room. The heater is made of a steel barrel with an opening for wood and yak dung, and a chimney made out of tin cans. It radiates heat so I sit close to it, under a poster of the Mona Lisa. Abba tunes play loudly over the lodge stereo system. "*See that girl, watch that scene, dig in the Dancing Queen...Friday night and the lights are low...*" The lodge owner's wife mimics words to the music as she tallies the food bill for the Australian group.

The tents of a group of English trekkers have been lined neatly outside the lodge, their porters and guides and now they begin celebrating the end of their trip. In no time they are deep into the liquor. Their compliant porters and guides have brought in drums and are singing Nepalese folk songs. As the party grows more boisterous, inebriated porters and clients bump into me as they dance about the room. I'd join them, but they're celebrating coming down from Everest Base Camp, and I still have the hard trek in front of me. With a worsening cold, the best thing for me is to get some rest. I nod goodnight to the owner and head for my tiny room, adjacent to the dining room. I put on my thermal underwear and slide into my sleeping bag, which I've spread atop the narrow sponge mattress. Only wooden planks separate me from the frolic in the dining room. Boots thud clumsily on wooden floorboards, just metres from my bed. I find my earplugs and shove them well into my ears. But it's almost dawn before the party ends and I can finally drift off to sleep.

3

Lukla to Monjo
Getting Started

In the morning I ask the lodge owner to recommend a porter to take my backpack. Within minutes, an enthusiastic porter is clasping my pressed palms within his. Chandra Rai stares at me with the fervour of a disciple. "I only need a porter for the two-day walk to Namche Bazaar," I tell him. "And then I will pay a third day for you to return to Lukla."

Chandra picks up my heavy pack using a tumpline over his head just behind his hairline while the bottom of the strap supports the backpack. He leans forward, allowing the back to help support the load and we head past the airfield. The runway nearly cuts through the village of Lukla, taking up most of one side while the few lodges and the post office occupy the other. Town and airport seem to be an integral piece, clinging tenaciously to a spur on the ridge. Cows and dogs wander about, as do porters, guides and trekkers. We pass the English group, now quite subdued with each member nursing a high altitude hangover, waiting at the airstrip for their flight out. The disassembled tents will be loaded onto the backs of porters and carried out to Jiri, before being trucked back to Kathmandu.

On the airport apron stacks of beer, rice, sugar and other goods accumulate in small mountains of their own before being dispersed onto the backs of porters to be carried up the trail. Cows, dogs and people on the airstrip scatter as three Twin Otters land in succession. Squads of hopeful freelance guides and would-be porters scrutinise the arriving passengers and hound prospective clients, the newly arrived trekkers easily identified by their wide-eyed stares as they mill about. There's a constant buzz of propellers thrashing the air as planes or helicopters land and take off, fuselages crammed with departing or arriving climbers. A Twin Otter perched at the top of the runway lurches forward as the pilot releases the brakes and the aircraft hurtles down the sloping runway. Almost by default, it is launched above the heavy clouds clogging the valley below. I linger to watch twenty or more flights arrive and take off, including three helicopters. Soon, the gravel airstrip will have a tarmac surface and even more Western trekkers will flock to the foot of the highest mountain in the world.

The only path through the village leads to Everest. Groups of men and boys play cards in the dirt or hover around a board game called *carom*. I stop for a few minutes and watch as the players flick plastic pucks expertly with a cocked finger to knock the discs into holes at the corners of the square table. The smooth wooden board is dusted with talcum powder to reduce the friction of the chips gliding across the surface. There are no women playing games, they are all working in the fields, or homes, or working in lodges.

A cluster of Tibetans sits by the wayside selling Tibetan carpets and cheap Made-in-China goods. The Tibetan traders are identifiable by their long hair interwoven with red beads curled over their heads and clumps of turquoise decorating their earlobes. In piles around them are brightly coloured bolts of material, imitation Nike running shoes, sweaters, fake North Face clothing. These traders look tough and they are. They have climbed over high passes to bring these goods out of Chinese-occupied Tibet into Nepal.

Beside the pathway a butcher sells slabs of meat from a gory carcass barely recognizable as a buffalo. Beneath the dismembered chunks of flesh a blue tarpaulin has turned purple with blood.

Six *zopkio*, crossbreeds between yaks and cows, lumber down the main flagstone thoroughfare oblivious to the fate of their distant relatives. Bulging trekking gear strapped to wooden saddles splayed across the zopkios' backs threaten unwary pedestrians. An earnest-looking backpacker with thick prescription glasses carefully studies the names of lodges as he walks. In his hand is an open copy of the Lonely Planet guidebook, his forefinger marking the page of lodge recommendations. Western, Chinese and Indian melodies filter from the teashops.

Scraggly cows chew plastic bags found in mounds of rubbish. Porters totter by, heavily laden with cases of tinned beer and plastic bottles of water. There is a constant ebb and flow of pedestrian traffic.

Ragged lines of trekkers with the thousand-metre stare of battle-weary soldiers descend to Lukla from Namche Bazaar. Their faces are burnished a deep brown except for the paleness around the eyes where sunglasses have protected skin from the sun. The men sport stubbles of beards and the women have that self-conscious air of the reluctantly unwashed. In stark contrast to the trekkers' grim demeanour are the smiling faces of their guides and porters, who are happy another trip is over and their pockets are about to be lined again. The few trekkers heading up into the mountains are conspicuous by their neat appearance and clean clothes. They walk tightly packed together, not a metre separating one from the other, as they file tidily out of Lukla, their even more smartly dressed Sherpa guides wearing the latest in Goretex and Maui Jims leading the way.

In the first hint of the hierarchy that exists up here, Chandra Rai says hello to the other Rais we pass, but not to the Sherpas. Historically, the Sherpas were the poorer relations, living at the upper limit of human habitation, growing potatoes in marginally productive fields at high altitudes, supplementing their meagre subsistence farming by working as porters carrying heavy loads for the first climbing expeditions that came to the Khumbu, or eking out a living as traders between Tibetans and the tribes lower down in Nepal.

Sherpa is a derivative from the Tibetan Shar-pa or 'people from the east' and the Sherpas almost certainly came from Eastern Tibet. Half a century ago *sherpa* became a generic term Western climbers to the region used to denote a porter. But more recently *sherpa* has the connotation of guide, rather than porter. There are few Sherpas carrying loads these days, unless they are young. Now it is the ethnic Rais, and the Tamangs, similar in feature to the Sherpas, and sometimes even the high-caste but often destitute Hindu Brahmins and the Chetris from lower down the valley who work as lowly porters. With so much money pouring into the high mountain areas, the once materially poor Sherpas are now at the top of the economic pile, many of them affluent enough to have secondary homes in Kathmandu.

Chandra Rai and I follow a group of trekkers with their Sherpa guide. The skies ahead are clear but dark grey clouds close in to the south. It feels good to be walking again. Despite the burden of a small daypack full of camera equipment, my back seems to be pain free, although stiff. The altitude headache from flying in to Lukla yesterday has gone, at least for now. We follow a caravan of *zopkio*, each animal loaded with a burlap bag of rice slung over either side of its spine. We meet another caravan carrying supplies and baggage for a trekking group. Tents, backpacks, steel tables, folding chairs and even a toilet seat, perch perilously on the backs of several animals. Chandra warns me to watch out as a *zopkio* with a rope through its nose tosses his horns at a passing trekker, catching him painfully on the leg. For a couple of hours a dog follows me, or leads the way, constantly looking over his shoulder to make sure I am there. These homeless dogs have learnt that trekking groups have surplus food, or even better, a kindly client who will take an indulgent interest in their well being for the duration of their trek.

Chandra picks up on my signals that I prefer to walk alone and in silence so we proceed in tandem, usually with him some distance out of sight further up the path. His English is rudimentary and it's hard work trying to converse with him and my Nepali isn't fluent enough to make it easy to communicate beside elementary instructions. Besides, I really don't want to distract myself from my introspections with idle chatter and niceties.

Crossing the river to several large lodges at Phakding, the trail from Lukla joins the track from Jiri. The first mountaineers had to walk almost all the way from Kathmandu to Everest. Decades later, they walked from the trailhead at Jiri, but nowadays there are fewer and fewer Western trekkers taking this more arduous route. Most, like me, fly in and out of Lukla, thereby cutting a couple of weeks off the overall time for the Everest trek. The short stretch of a couple of hours from Lukla to Phakding is lined with lodges, teahouses, and shops catering to tourists and their retinue of porters and guides.

A young Sherpa girl descends the path carrying a full *doko* basket on her back, the weight of the load supported by a tumpline extending from the bottom of the basket over the top of her head. Three Sherpa boys see her coming. They slyly pick up a skull-sized rock and place it in her basket as she passes by. They laugh when she discovers the rock, but so does she.

Many of the lodges have wooden shacks marked *TOILET* on weathered doors. These are cantilevered over the hillside atop a pile of pine needles that act as compost as well as alleviate the stench of human refuse. It's not a coincidence they are adjacent to a vegetable garden with this steady flow of free fertilizer. Some latrines are built directly over an occupied pigpen.

Today, I will walk only some hours, as far as Monjo, the last village before the gateway to Sagarmatha National Park. I choose one of the lodges, the Kalaish Lodge, although Chandra Rai tries to persuade me to stay at another. He drops off my backpack and we agree to meet in the morning. He obviously has a lodge that he prefers to stay at. Our arrangement is that I pay him a lump sum per day for his services and he sorts out his own accommodation and meals.

Inside the lodge just before the park entrance, I discover an American group who are heading up and a German group who are heading down. Unlike the Annapurnas, individual trekkers are the minority on the Everest Base Camp walk. I sit at a table in the dining room, my presence made obvious by a hacking cough and a pile of toilet paper accumulating beside me. The dining room, like the one at Lukla, has the traditional layout and furnishings of a Sherpa home: the windowed walls lined with benches covered in Tibetan rugs, all facing trunk-sized wooden tables. A Sherpa with a film star's good looks walks in wearing a sheepskin jacket. I tell him, enunciating clearly, so that he should understand me, what I would like to have for dinner. He takes my order, and replies in perfect English. Embarrassed by his flawless accent I ask him how he learned to speak English so well.

"I went to school for eight years in Dharmsala, in India," he says, sitting down beside me. "I could only speak the Sherpa language when I went there, and I had to learn Hindi, Tibetan, and English. My father was a Tibetan but he left when I was two and my mother died when I had been at the school for two years." He points at a house across the pathway. "That's where I was born. My uncle was a *sirdar* for climbing expeditions and he found a German to sponsor me for nine years. When my sponsor died, I had to leave the school. I was seventeen years old and by then I couldn't speak my own Sherpa language. I had to learn it all over again. But it's not very different from Tibetan, more like a dialect."

In a short time, he tells me his entire history. His name is Tsering Chombi Sherpa. He began working for trekking expeditions as a porter before he was promoted to kitchen boy, then cook, then assistant *sirdar*, and finally *sirdar,* boss of a climbing or trekking expedition, a role traditionally held by Sherpas. He worked for Tiger Mountain for twelve years as a *sirdar* and was head *sirdar* for Wilderness Travel. He doesn't look old enough to have done all this.

"Now I have spent this year working on building this new dining room and running the lodge with my wife," he tells me.

"So that's how come your English is so good?"

He shrugs. "I spent a lot of time in America too."

"And the lodge is all yours?"

"Since I had no parents at such a young age, I worked for six years to save the money for breaking stones, the wood, the cement, the windows," he says. "Now I'm looking forward to leading trekking groups again. Besides, we need the extra money. We have two boys, ten and sixteen, in English boarding school in Kathmandu." As he takes my dinner order I see his handwriting is quite beautiful. "Our busy season is October and November and a little bit December. Then January and February is slow, and the trekkers start coming again in March and April. Just some years ago the number of trekkers went up thirty per cent in one year, but now because of the Maoists there are not so many as before. Our best customers are Everest climbers, they have the biggest budget but how much they spend depends on the group leader. This year there are fewer Everest expeditions because the Nepalese Government raised the fees for climbing Everest to $70,000 for a permit. Now some Everest expeditions go to Tibet because it is cheaper."

"Have you climbed Everest?" I ask.

"No."

"Could you?"

He laughs at my question. "Any Sherpa could climb Everest given a chance. Sherpas will even pay their *sirdar* to select them to be a high altitude sherpa."

"A bribe."

He shrugs. "That's how it is done."

I know he's telling the truth. Sherpas on Everest expeditions maybe get one thousand five hundred dollars each for equipment, plus three hundred rupees a day plus all the food they can eat. After Camp three to five, they get a bonus of two or three hundred dollars a day to set up those camps. To be a high altitude sherpa they might pay the *sirdar* five thousand rupees, or give him a down jacket.

"And you think most Sherpas could get to the top of Everest?"

He nods his head and smiles. "No problem."

More than three hundred foreigners have made it to the top of Everest, with a lot of fanfare. Some fifteen hundred Sherpas have made it to the top, most of them having carried heavy supplies on the way up there, but they have climbed Everest with the minimum of publicity. One has made it to the top of Everest without oxygen fourteen times. One made it to the top of Everest in less than eleven hours. Another remained on top of Everest for twenty-one hours. While many Westerners have died in the attempt to get to the top of Everest, even more Sherpas have died getting their clients up there.

Chombi's wife walks in, talking on a cordless phone to someone in Namche Bazaar about a group booking. Not so long ago trekking groups sent a guide ahead to book the rooms for their clients. Now phoning ahead is a lot easier. Cell phones and solar panels exist side-by-side with ramshackle rooms, pit latrines, gravity-fed water, rudimentary fires in steel barrels for heating and no electricity. The mixture of new technology and primitive living conditions in this rudimentary setting is bewildering.

I leave Chombi and his wife to arrange their business and step outside to wander around Monjo. Climbing up to the top end of the village I pass a signboard requesting donations for the Utche Chhloeling Monastery. A woman in traditional dress sees me read the information board.

"No good," she tells me.

"Why?" I ask, but she ignores my question. A large padlocked wooden box sits in anticipation of donations from passing trekkers. I look up to the spur of a hill where the *gompa* monastery is to be built. It is hard to see what is up there, but there is a massive prayer wheel. Its prayer flags flutter in the wind. I am curious, but suffering from the high altitude I have little energy to climb any higher to spin the wheel to propel the enclosed prayers to the gods. I head back down to the lodge.

Although it is dark by the time I return, the dining room is well lit. Chinese solar panels carried by Tibetans over six and a half thousand-metres high passes provide electricity for light bulbs. Everyone coughs, especially the descending Germans. While we sit huddled on Tibetan carpets on bench seats with our backs exposed to the cold windows, the wiser Nepalese guides and porters sit huddled together for warmth around the space heater in the centre of the room.

An Irishman next to me gives me a throat lozenge for my throat and tells me he walked up from the trailhead at Jiri.

"Took seven days to reach Phakding," he says. "Most nights I was the only trekker in the village. Hardly saw anyone the whole way. And then suddenly at Phakding, there were hordes of tourists, the lodges were bigger and fancier and more numerous, and everyone, including the Nepalese people, were more aggressive."

The American group is overnighting in the lodge, and are excited about their trip up to Everest and Gokyo. They have paid a flat fee to the trekking company and their guide arranges and pays for all the food and lodging in lodges along the way. For the service of having a guide find a lodge and pay their bills, they have paid a substantial premium. I listen vaguely to their conversation. It's good to be alone with my thoughts, and my notebook, but strange also to be myself. Ever since I broke my back, I've been living with Annabel. Although I wanted this time on my own, to think about things and re-establish my sense of independence, it's already an unfamiliar feeling keeping my thoughts entirely to myself.

For the first time in months I let my mind wander freely, pulling the threads together of a disparate life. Born in Canada of British parents, my father was posted to a series of countries as a foreign correspondent. Before my fourth birthday I had left Canada to live in Hong Kong, followed by India, Kenya, and Malaysia. I had attended seven schools before my fifteenth birthday. By seventeen I had attended two more. The itinerant lifestyle became the norm for my siblings and me and we forged a bond of friendship out of necessity. Inevitably, we became insular. It became too hurtful to make new friends only to be torn apart with a complete shift in lifestyles from one country to the next. Sometimes we went to boarding schools. My brother and two sisters and I became close friends because we were a unit that was never broken apart. Even if we were separated from our parents, we shared the same boarding schools in Scotland and Singapore. In India, when I was eight and my brother was six, we were the only non-Indians at boarding school in Old Delhi.

The oldest of the four of us children, I tended to be the most serious, the most responsible. I was rarely in trouble. I studied hard, didn't party, never smoked or did drugs and didn't drink at all during adolescence and not to excess for most of my life. During my undergraduate years, while studying philosophy, I was an innocent. By twenty-one I was studying post-graduate economics and at the age of twenty-four, after a couple of years in banking, I was recruited through the Canadian Foreign Service to a two-year secondment in East Africa with the United Nations Development Programme. Completing my contract with the UN, I remained in Tanzania, obtained my pilot's licence, bought a Cessna 182 and started a safari business in the Selous Game Reserve.

Meanwhile life back home had changed. We had two homes in effect, in London and Toronto. My father gave up being a foreign correspondent and then wrote two bestsellers in one year. My parents moved to Bermuda. While I was running and flying around the East African bush, my siblings had followed my parents to Bermuda where they found jobs and one sister and my brother married Bermudians and settled down to have families. From being the most serious of my siblings, I was now the eccentric of the family, camped in the largest game reserve in Africa, living a life on the edge, with no prospects of settling down in sight.

I'd always admired Kevin's drive and ambition. He vowed as a teenager that he'd be a millionaire by the time he was thirty. There was no reason not to believe he would become very wealthy. He worked hard, and when he died, he was on the point of taking it easy. By contrast I have shied from material success. Money didn't hold as much value to me as my independence.

My brother had come to visit me in Tanzania. It was one of the best times we ever had together, when I felt genuinely close to Kevin. It was an expense-free trip for him and I pulled no punches, flying him around the country in my plane with the added luxury of one of my Land Rovers and a driver to meet us at airstrips in the Serengeti, Ngorogoro, Lake Manyara as well as our own exclusive time in the Selous Game Reserve. It was a magical occasion and I was so proud to show him my adopted life of adventure.

By the time I was thirty I had had the rare opportunity to live in a genuine African wilderness, an area that was so large it had remained pristine. But I had also been dangerously sick with cerebral malaria, hepatitis, tick bite fever and dengue fever. Twice, poisonous snakes bit me. Always thin and wiry, I was now alarmingly skinny. With foreign exchange controls in Tanzania at the time, there were no spare parts for planes and aircraft were dropping out of the skies with regularity. My own Cessna, Tango Bravo Whiskey, was the oldest aircraft in the country and I became increasingly aware that flying over the largest reserve in Africa, living dangerously in the bush in a country with only rudimentary medical care, was pushing my luck. I did have an engine failure once and spent the night out in the bush with no prospect of anyone finding me if I couldn't get it started again. I had had numerous close calls with animals and other misadventures and was rapidly using up my nine lives. I was also fed up of tourists, the major downside to running a tourist business in the African bush.

Increasingly I assigned more and more of the duties to my African staff until the only trips I undertook myself with tourists were the early morning walking safaris, which were inherently dangerous. I became paranoid that I was going to die in Africa before I turned thirty, and I really wasn't ready to die. Because of foreign exchange controls, although I had plenty of Tanzanian shillings, I was penniless as far as the real world was concerned. When the Tanzanian authorities made it clear that they intended to take the camp over, I decided not to push my luck any further and despite objections from my partners, I left Tanzania to return to Canada. Some months later one of my partners died from injuries incurred in the Selous.

It was hard when I returned to the real world to make the adjustment. I never talked about my safari days. It was too hurtful for one thing, and for another, no one could really relate to the lifestyle I'd led. However, all my family had come out to Tanzania to visit at one time or another and they became the link to the existence I had left behind. Kevin went out of his way to introduce me to his friends and to open doors for me in Bermuda. But Bermuda was too small after living large.

I needed to make money so I became a financial consultant in New York and Toronto and quickly made more money than I felt I needed. After four years I quit to work for a Canadian charity undertaking long-term development work in Africa and Asia. I travelled some six to eight months overseas annually, visiting the isolated communities of the grassroots villagers who were the recipients of our aid. Whenever I had the chance, I tried to get down to Bermuda to visit my family and Kevin was always there to meet me at the airport.

Then, after falling in love with a Norwegian and a stint living in Norway running two adventure businesses and working as a consultant for the Norwegian and Swedish overseas aid programmes in Africa, I decided to move to Bermuda and use it as a base to start writing about my travels. Strangely, although moving to Bermuda I was physically closer to Kevin, the distance between us was never greater.

I have tried not to feel guilty after my brother died, but I realize also that sense of guilt is part of this journey I am taking with the envelope. Despite being godfather to his daughter, Kevin and I saw each other less and less although we lived on a small island. We moved in different circles and grew apart.

The last time I saw Kevin alive was his birthday. I went to visit him. He was in bed, sick. It was the longest time I'd spent time with him alone since I'd moved to Bermuda. I joked that because he was bedridden, he couldn't get away from me. He told me he thought he had the flu but he'd been vomiting as well and although he'd been sick in bed for some weeks he still refused to see a doctor.

Countless times in the weeks after his death, I played it out in my mind, how I should have asked Annabel, a doctor, to go over and check up on Kevin when he said he'd been feeling sick. Any doctor doing a basic examination would have realised there was something drastically wrong. Annabel would have had him hospitalised. But I didn't ask her to visit him.

Despite being sick, and against his wife's wishes, Kevin went on an important weekend business trip to the United States.

Three days later my sister's husband telephoned. "Kevin's had a heart attack," he told me.

"Is he okay?" I replied.

"He dead."

I dropped the phone on the floor as if it had scalded my hand. They found his body in his hotel room on the Monday morning. I can't imagine a lonelier death than an anonymous hotel room in the United States. He died of a massive heart attack. He had probably had a minor attack weeks earlier and that was why he had been feeling so unwell.

Days later, my sister Jackie and I went to the airport to wait for the plane carrying his coffin. It was the saddest day I can remember. We sat at a high point on the Bermuda shoreline and watched the flight coming in, knowing his body was on board. Kevin, the one who usually came to pick me up at the airport when I visited Bermuda.

After Kevin died, I tried as much as possible to stand in for him. I took his son to baseball games on the weekend, read bedtime stories to his daughter. Six weeks after he died I was in a motorbike accident and my life collapsed around me.

In the middle of the night I wake up, alone in my room. It takes me a few seconds to remember where I am, high in the Himalayas. I have to pee. I've been drinking copious amounts of water to allow my kidneys to flush out the build-up of carbonates that contribute to altitude sickness. The bulb on my flashlight works briefly, then burns out. I don't have a spare. In complete darkness, I feel my way to the door, and then along the corridor walls, down the creaking stairs to the front doors where I unlatch an interior wooden beam across the heavy plank doors and exit into the village pathway to urinate against a stone wall. It is almost a full moon and the valley is cast in moonlight. It is eerily quiet and peaceful. The only sound is the Dudh Kosi, the highest river in the world, rumbling through the valley bottom.

⚜

4

Arriving in Namche Bazaar

Early the next morning I cough up globules of bright yellow mucus. The top of my sleeping bag is so wet that water droplets run down the sides. The windows are covered in condensation. Frost lies on the ground outside and, for the first time, the sky is clear of clouds.

Rather than rush off, I tell Chandra Rai that we will have a late start this morning and I wait until the German and American groups have gone. With an empty lodge and time on his hands, Chombi shows me around his village. Beyond the narrow corridor of trekking traffic, there is life outside tourism. We walk around Monjo, through alleyways, past stone houses, alongside stone walls to a four hundred-year old *gompa*. Every traditional village here has a Buddhist temple or *gompa*. I tell Chombi about the woman's comments yesterday evening when I had stopped in front of the sign requesting donations from passing tourists.

"Why did she say, *No good, no good?*" I ask.

"People say the lama keeps the money for himself, instead of building a new *gompa*,' Chombi says, apparently reticent to reveal this bit of information. He gestures around a courtyard as we enter. "But this is the real *gompa* for the village. This temple is four hundred years old." We look at a dilapidated old building, which doesn't appear anything like a temple, monastery, or *gompa*. Somebody's rundown house, maybe. We walk inside, into what looks like a derelict barn on the ground floor, up a dark creaking wooden stairway and into a sombre room. There are two beds at the end of the room, with large clay fireplace-stove, pots and pans and other paraphernalia. Two Tibetan women hover around the burning stove. Sitting in front of the fire is a young man who I assume is Japanese, judging from his appearance. Chombi introduces me to the two women.

"And this is Tam," he adds, "A schoolteacher assigned to our local school. He lives here."

"You sleep in the *gompa*?" I ask.

Tam laughs at the notion.

"Well, they tried to persuade me to sleep in the actual temple room, which is just through there," he says. "But I found it a bit spooky sleeping in a room with Buddha. So I sleep in the corner bed there and Ama, the older woman, sleeps in the other bed." Noticing my look of disbelief, he adds, "A bit different from the bedroom at my parent's place in Ottawa, that's for sure, eh."

The two Sherpa women are bent over double as they prepare Tam's breakfast. The top of the clay stove, and the sides, are lined with flattened five-gallon soybean oilcans.

"I pay three thousand six hundred dollars for the privilege of teaching here as a volunteer teacher," Tam explains. This isn't a precursor to a complaint. "But it's worth it, eh. They look after my food, board, and most of my expenses while I am here for the three months. Back home I'm a computer programmer. But I wanted to live another life. I could have gone trekking, but that wouldn't be a fair assessment of this world. So I searched the Internet and here I am, sleeping in a four hundred-year old *gompa* with an old lady, and teaching Sherpa kids English in the local school. Existence here definitely circulates around the trekking business, although, off the trail, it's not so important. The households around here might grow vegetables and then go up to Namche Bazaar early, three or four in the morning on a Saturday, to sell their produce, but that's really their only contact with tourism."

"Do your students attend school regularly?" I ask, as I accept a steaming hot cup of tea from the old lady.

"Sometimes the older kids don't show up for school because they are helping out harvesting potatoes, beans, corn, hay," Tam tells me. "Sometimes they carry younger siblings on their backs to the classes to look after because their parents work in the fields."

The woman washes a teacup under a faucet above a sink. Tam laughs when he sees me observing this modern convenience.

"My one daily chore is to fetch water every morning in buckets and fill the barrel above the faucet," he says. "That way, we have what appears to be running water for the rest of the day."

The younger of the two women serves Chombi and me another cup of tea. On a bench seat beside the window, the older woman sits happily, mumbling as she thumbs through her prayer beads.

"*O Mani Padme Hum,*" she mumbles aloud the prayer or mantra that Tibetan Buddhists say aloud or to themselves, invoking the blessings of Chenrezig, the Buddha of Compassion.

"At least she doesn't snore," Tam jokes. "But she clangs symbols and chants prayers until she falls asleep. In the morning she wakes me by banging drums in the *gompa* room next door."

"And this *gompa* is more popular than the new monastery asking for donations?" I ask.

"This *is* the village *gompa*, there is no other *gompa*," Tam assures me, affirming what Chombi had also stated. "The villagers don't know where the money to build the new *gompa* is disappearing. The lama who requests the money had a good, famous lama for a father. But they've been building that *gompa* for fifteen years and all that's up there is a prayer wheel, which was taken from further up the valley. Still, a lot of trekkers give him donations."

As Tam eats breakfast, the old lady shows me into the *gompa* proper, with its antique statues of the Buddha. I leave a small donation and Chombi and I continue on our way. We walk through the village, passing the lodge which sits above Chombi's.

"The owner of that lodge is married to an American woman," he tells me with reverence. "He has a green card and his Sherpani wife runs his lodge."

"He has two wives?" I ask.

Chombi smiles. "I don't know," he replies diplomatically, "but he has a green card."

The green card, or green light to the United States and financial security, is the Holy Grail for the Sherpas in the Khumbu.

We make our way up to the school, a flat piece of cleared ground with simple buildings lined along one edge. Tam is already there, waiting as the children come running up the hill. They form several neat queues in front of the school buildings. An older child blows a whistle whilst leading the others in callisthenics to get their little bodies and lungs going before they sing the national anthem.

The older children hand out fluoride pills to the younger ones while a helicopter flies overhead, the first of the Everest scenic flights from Kathmandu, scooting up the valley to circle around Namche Bazaar before heading back.

School begins at ten. A few stragglers appear as others head into their respective classrooms where they sing songs for several minutes on a beautiful crisp and clear day.

"I'm going to miss this," Tam tells me. Just then a man appears over the lip of the flat schoolyard and Tam points him out. "That teacher comes from Namche Bazaar every day, returning home every evening," he says with great respect.

It will take me a good three hours to get up to Namche. I can't imagine commuting the distance both ways every day.

Chombi leads me to the top of the spur where the new *gompa* is supposed to be. Sure enough, the only structure is the old prayer wheel, and a small office where the lama sits, collecting donations. He isn't there. There's a pile of stones, ostensibly for the foundations of the temple, but nothing else. From the perspective below, the prayer flags, the old building containing the prayer wheel and the office of the lama, it looks as if there could be a *gompa*. But there isn't. And yet even Jamie's Everest guidebook indicates a *gompa* is here.

Back at his lodge, Chombi gets on with his day. Despite instructions to Chandra Rai, my young porter, that we would be having a late morning start, he smiles profusely and tells me he is just about to have his *dal bhaat*, his lentils and rice. He will meet me somewhere on the trail ahead. It's a cloudless sky and my mood is upbeat. I walk to the top of the village and pay the six hundred and fifty-rupee fee to enter Sagarmatha National Park. From there, it is a quick steep descent back down to the river. I cross one long suspension bridge festooned with prayer flags and abandoned *kata* scarves and then walk back to the other side on another suspension bridge. The Dudh Kosi rushes by milky and turquoise-coloured from the suspended fine powder ground down by the glaciers far up the valley. Porters have congregated in sandy spaces between boulders to cook their rice and lentils and curried potatoes, blue smoke curling from their fires.

Trekking companies refer to how environmentally correct they are and how they have less impact on the ecology of the area because they use kerosene to cook their clients' food. What they tend to ignore is that an army of porters accompanies the trekking group and the porters often cook their own meals over wood fires along the path. Of all the pedestrian traffic walking up and down these trails, it is most likely the porters rather than the trekkers who are guilty of leaving rubbish in their wake. This is not so much because the porters don't care, but because they don't know any better. It seems to me to be ecologically friendlier to use lodges, rather than tents and furniture that have been carried backwards and forwards up and down the trails by an army of porters that must be fed. Besides, lodge owners are more likely to be aware of their own fragile environment than outsiders passing through their villages. One hears about the garbage on the Everest trail, and certainly there are places along the route from Lukla to Namche which do look like rubbish tips. Signs sponsored by WWF or Sagarmatha Pollution Control Committee indicating *Rubbish Dump*, tend to be places with sheer drops towards the river where the plastic and other rubbish accumulates, out of sight and out of mind. But when the wind blows, the rubbish is scattered everywhere.

It is not only the cloudless sky that has uplifted my spirits. The lack of lodges, teahouses and shops inside the park entrance gives a bit of a wilderness feel to the walk. I am within the park now where there are limitations to the number of lodges or teahouses that can be built. At the confluence of two rivers, I cross another swaying suspension bridge festooned with colourful prayer flags. One river is the Imja Khola leading up to Everest. I stop on the swaying bridge to look up the side valley towards Everest. The walls are so steep the valley seems impregnable, which is precisely why travellers must zigzag up along the ridge of the Bhote Kosi, up to Namche, circumventing the impenetrable gorge entrance to the Everest and Gokyo valleys.

From the suspension bridge there are a few steep switchbacks. At the corner of one, three descending trekkers tell me where I can get a glimpse of Everest. Arriving at a well-scuffed zigzag in the trail, I can indeed see a discombobulated snow-covered peak peering over the tips of trees and closer ridges. Climbing up the steep hill to Namche, sweat pouring off me, I become dehydrated, having totally miscalculated the opportunities to fill my water bottle en route. Towards the top of the climb, I finally find a source of water. I fill my bottle and drop in an iodine tablet before continuing. My progress is slow because of the debilitating effects of high altitude. Already, each step is a deliberate effort and requires a pause every few minutes to regain my breath.

Two porters overtake me carrying *dokos* filled with fresh meat they will sell in Namche. Each basket contains recognisable chunks of buffalo. With not much more to occupy my mind, I try to categorise the trekkers on the route and divide them into two basic categories: Those Going Up, and Those Going Down. Those Going Up are recognisable because we all look clean and excited. Those Going Down aren't so immaculate, or enthusiastic. Trekkers can be divided into Group People who can be sub-divided into Tent People, Teahouse People and the Ice Pick People. The Tent People are supposed to sleep in groups in tents. The Teahouse People sleep in groups in teahouses. The Ice Pick People are groups climbing trekking peaks like Island Peak. They have a retinue of guides and porters to carry everything, just like the other Tent People. But the Ice Pick People carry their ice picks attached conspicuously to the outside of their daypacks with crampons jangling below, despite the fact that there is no likelihood of using their ice picks or crampons along this stretch. We are after all a thousand and more metres below the snow line. But by displaying their climbing equipment, plebeian trekkers like myself are reminded that the Ice Pick People are climbers, climbing a peak, and not to be confused with the those of us whose goals are only to go up to hackneyed Kala Pattar overlooking Everest Base Camp.

Just like the Group People, Individual Trekkers can also be classified into sub-species too. Some, like myself, have a porter. Some have a guide and no porter. Some have a guide and a porter, which is a bit redundant. And some carry their own packs. Those carrying their own packs can be further divided into two groups: those who carry their own packs because they are purists and are used to carrying their own packs in countries where porters don't exist. They tend to be fit and strong, male and female. The others carry their own packs because they can't afford to pay for a porter, or, if they can afford to pay for a porter, won't. I have a porter now because I promised everyone at home that I would take a porter, given my condition since my accident. As it is, just carrying my daypack with my cameras and lenses is enough of a strain on my recuperating back.

In this overall hierarchical ordering of trekkers, I am the lowest of the low. Firstly, I'm one of Those Going Up, not down, so I don't have any knowledge or information to impart, just endless questions. From the Nepalese point of view, I am not a Group People, with a retinue of employees, so I'm not splurging on the experience, an indication that I am not as flush with cash. To the Nepalese, travelling on my own like this, I could be one of those insolvent travellers taking a year off, eking out my daily expenses to a few dollars a day.

Even amongst the Individual Trekkers, I have no status because I'm not carrying my own pack: I have a Nepalese porter who is half my size and weight doing all the hard work. Even if you don't get kudos from the Nepalese for being an Individual Trekker, there's a certain amount of satisfaction staring down the Group People while heavily loaded with one's own backpack. So, I have no plaudits from either group. I'm at the bottom of the ladder.

The first buildings of Namche appear through the pine trees from around a corner in the path. Climbing higher, I am suddenly over the lip of the ridge facing the bowl-like amphitheatre that contains Namche Bazaar. It's an unexpected apparition. In my imagination I thought Namche was at the confluence of two rivers. It sits in fact, perched high above a steep drop to the Bhote River. Once a natural amphitheatre of terraced potato fields, it is sown now with lodges. Coloured prayer flags flutter gaily from the surrounding ridge tops.

Walking through the centre of Namche is akin to strolling through the Thamel tourist district in Kathmandu. Shops crowd the narrow pathway, displaying just about everything and anything one might need for the trek up to Everest Base Camp. Thermal underwear, North Face and Patagonia clothes, both genuine and cheap Chinese imitations, hang from coat hangers or hooks. Pitons, crampons, ice screws, thermoses, sleeping bags, tents, sweaters, woollen hats, gloves and socks are piled high in boxes. For the Group People who have the luxury of porters to carry all their local purchases, are innumerable "Tibetan" artefacts displayed on wooden tables. Some are authentic, but many "Tibetan" items are made in India, Thailand, or Kathmandu. There is an air of excitement, like the big city, but there are no vehicles here. In fact, besides the prayer wheels, there's nothing else with a wheel within some weeks walk. Apart from the planes landing at Lukla, these steep mountains preclude the use of anything rolling around on wheels.

In the centre of the village I stroll by a couple of sweet-smelling bakeries, and then two ramshackle disco bars replete with flashing lights, poolrooms, and a sauna. Perhaps most incongruous of all are the cyber cafés where I can send e-mails. Tomorrow is Saturday, market day. Wandering around the narrow alleys are Tibetan traders, tough men with long hair curled in topknots above their heads, turquoise in their earlobes and padded thermal trousers and traditional sheepskin jackets. They seem slightly bewildered by the attractions of Namche Bazaar.

I'm tempted to collapse in one of the lodges in lower Namche, instead of bothering to haul myself up the extra distance to the Panorama Lodge. Although it is only a couple of hundred metres up the path, the effort to get there is out of proportion to the distance. Nevertheless I keep walking, slowly, out of breath, and with a bit of a headache, up the right flank of the bowl-like depression that forms Namche, to a lodge perched above the others.

The first person I meet is a woman hanging washing on the clothesline. She wears the traditional Sherpa outfit, a long skirt with a multi-coloured apron at the front. She beams at me, as if happy to see a prodigal son return to the fold. I ask her if she has a room for me.

"You are Andrew?"

"Yes," I reply.

"I am Lhakpa."

Perhaps Chombi gave her a description of me when he phoned up to book me a room. She hands me the key. Chandra Rai takes my bag and I follow, up to the third floor. On the first and second floors are flush porcelain toilets, and porcelain urinals as well, a luxury rarely witnessed in the high Himalayas. It's a relief to change out of clothes wet with perspiration, into dry ones. Steam rises from the damp clothes as I toss them onto the bed. Chandra remains in my room with an expression on his face befitting someone about to be shot. I pay him what we had agreed in Lukla: two days' salary, plus another day's salary to walk back to Lukla. Despite giving him a handsome tip, I feel dreadful dismissing him.

"I no go Everest Base Camp?" he asks plaintively.

"No Chandra, I want to stay here for several days."

I want to explore, give my body a chance to adapt to the high altitude. Namche is already three and a half thousand metres high, or eleven and a half thousand feet.

"I wait," he answers.

"I don't know how long I will stay in Namche."

I try to be forceful about this. I could easily keep him, but I'd prefer an older porter, and one not quite so ingratiating. Chandra sometimes crowds my space with his overbearing willingness to please me.

I go down to the dining room, identical to the one in Monjo. Three sides are glass, providing views of Namche below and the mountains to the west, although there is no view of the high Himalayas, which are tucked behind the amphitheatre ridge. Bench seats line three walls of the dining room, in front of which are a line of trunk-sized tables. The room is cosy, a home-away-from-home. It is also immaculately clean. The floors have been oiled, and even the iron space heater in the middle of the large room has been oiled so that it does not turn rusty. The fourth wall includes the entrance, the door into the kitchen, and glass-faced cabinets full of beer, whiskey, wine, champagne, cigarettes, chocolate, and "yak-wool" sweaters, gloves and hats.

A young Tamang girl takes my late lunch order, a bowl of soup and a plate of French fries. Chandra comes into the dining room and hovers around with a hangdog look.

It's difficult enjoying my meal when he stands in front of me, waiting expectantly. My guilt in letting him go is exacerbated by the knowledge that the soup I'm eating costs almost a fifth of his daily wage. He smiles at me, but his eyes are sad.

"I go now?" he asks.

"Yes." I've got to be firm about this.

"I go Lukla now?"

"Yes."

"You no want porter now?"

"No."

"No want porter?" he confirms.

"No." I eat my soup. "I stay Namche now."

"After you want porter?"

Even if I did want him, I might cross the Cho La pass from the Everest Valley to Gokyo. The pass is five and a half thousand metres over a glacier. He doesn't have the requisite clothes with him.

"No, I don't need a porter, thanks Chandra."

"I run go Lukla now?"

"Yes."

With Lhakpa hovering around, Chandra Rai disappears. I feel bad, but I have to be resolute about what I want this trip to be, for me, not for someone else. With my back still recovering from a shattered vertebra, I have to have a porter, but I want one whose presence will be unobtrusive. I want a porter who will allow me to feel that I'm on my own.

The Tamang girl brings me French Fries. She giggles and smiles and throws me coquettish looks over her shoulder. Lhakpa's husband, Sherap, walks in with a cordless telephone at his ear, taking a booking from a trekking group on the way up from Lukla. With his left hand, he twists the few strands of his moustache as he concentrates on the detailed requirements of the group.

The sun disappears. Still addicted to being clean, I order a hot shower, with water heated by a kerosene burner. For a couple of dollars, I can have thirty-litre's worth of a hot shower. On my way down to the shower stall, pragmatically located beneath the kitchen where the water is being heated, I pass a heavy curtain hanging from a doorway. From the other side of the curtain, I can hear monks praying. I wonder if the room is a *choikan*, or prayer room. I stop to listen. The chanting is soothing, otherworldly. I draw the curtain aside to find a small cubicle with a computer on a table, instead of a large room full of monks. Microsoft Windows marquees glide across the screen of the monitor as Tibetan chants float out from two adjacent speakers. Sherap comes out from the kitchen twiddling the hairs of his moustache.

"You want to send an e-mail, or a fax?"

I had been convinced that there were a bunch of monks praying inside the room.

"You bought the computer so your clients could send e-mails home?" I ask incredulously.

"My son is at university in New York," he explains. "I bought the computer because it is easier to communicate with him. Much cheaper than fax or telephone."

Outside, cords of wood for the kitchen fire are unloaded from two *zopkio*, wood that legally must have come from outside the park boundary. The stove itself is a clay-mud oven fuelled by wood and yak dung. Mind-boggling how this high tech stuff exists side by side with what is, still, a very basic life-style.

I manage to make the shower last several minutes by turning the faucet so that only a trickle comes out. Clean and refreshed, I return to my room, which I discover is next to a huge prayer room complete with a statue of the Buddha and a wall lined with prayer books. Looking outside the window I see mist has set in, and through the mist I see the electric lights of Namche.

Unpacked, I dress in warm clothes and head downstairs. Infrared sensors detect my movement and automatically switch on electric lights. Standing outside the main part of the lodge I stop to listen. Namche is a natural amphitheatre, magnifying the sounds of yak bells, dogs barking, people yelling or whistling at their yaks or *zopkio*s. The mist clears above momentarily and through the gap I glimpse the summit of a snow-covered peak washed in the last rays of sunlight. This luminescent apparition is so far above, it doesn't seem as if it could possibly be connected to the ground. I watch until the peak disappears into the mist again and then the valley below fades away so that Namche seems to be perched over a void. Within a minute, the village is entirely engulfed in the thick mist.

In the kitchen I ask Sherap, who is still grooming his moustache, why there is electricity here, and yet I don't see any wire or poles. He laughs at the question.

"All underground," he says.

I am amazed. Only wealthy neighbourhoods in the Western world can afford to bury this unsightly infrastructure.

"Where's the electricity come from?"

"A hydropower station at Thame, built by the Austrians," he tells me. "It provides electricity to Namche, and the villages around. Lhakpa's brother is one of the technicians responsible for it's upkeep. He was trained in Austria."

Similarly, the Annapurna Circuit, in the Annapurnas to the west, is almost totally electrified now with small hydropower units.

Unfortunately, in the Annapurnas, it sometimes seems the aluminium electrical poles are installed in the most visually intrusive of places. Electrification, like cement walls and corrugated tin roofs, are for most Nepalese symbols of development, but for Westerners they often destroy the aesthetic qualities of the medieval villages we pass through. By contrast, the buried cables of the Everest region are a measure of the degree to which Western ideas and technology have permeated the Khumbu.

In my mind's eye, Namche Bazaar was a rustic Sherpa village with a few basic lodges catering to climbing expeditions and trekkers. But this is beyond my expectations. Admittedly, there are no vehicles of any kind, which gives Namche a certain medieval charm. But otherwise, Namche Bazaar is more Westernised than I could have imagined. Straddling the bowl that is the entry to Everest Base Camp and the Gokyo Valley, all trekkers have to pass through Namche Bazaar, a major staging point for Everest and the last place to stock up on supplies.

Sherap sits down in the dining room with a computer printout of a long list of telephone calls. He tells me Chombi from Monjo is coming up tomorrow and he and Sherap have to work out which long distance calls are his, and which are Chombi's, patched in from Monjo to Namche. It is not clear what their relationship is although it appears to be purely business. Clearly Sherap would rather talk to me than work out his phone bills. We are alone.

"How did you manage to afford such a big lodge?" I ask. It's one of the biggest, and most impressive lodges here. It must have some twenty plus rooms in the adjacent three-storey building.

"My family is from Namche, so I have land here. I took a private bank loan of one and a half million rupees to build the lodge and in three years I paid off the loan. Now I have expenses of my twenty-four year old son studying computer science in New York, and a daughter in secondary English boarding school in Kathmandu." He pulls at the few unruly strands of moustache.

"Do you think your son will come back to Namche after studying in New York?"

"Yeah."

"Are you sure?"

'I am sure," he says nodding.

"And you can afford to pay your son's fees and expenses?"

"He also has an American friend sponsoring him," Sherap replies.

"Do you have any brothers or sisters?" I ask.

"Thirteen," he says. "My father was a trader. He died crossing a pass when he was sixty. My mother and father had already split up, so I worked as a porter first. Then I was a waiter at the Hotel Everest View. Then I was on the first Italian expedition. After, I did small jobs at Tiger Mountain until nineteen-eighty, and then worked as a guide, then as *sirdar.* And now I am the local director of Butterfield and Robinson."

I too know Butterfield and Robinson and their luxury guided biking and hiking trips. "You never did an Everest expedition?" I ask Sherap.

He shakes his head. "My wife didn't like climbing expeditions. Many relatives have died on them. I went to America, once, as a guest to train for climbing. But when I came back my wife said no. At that time I was sorry not to climb, but now I am glad because I am still alive."

"What do you think of the Everest expeditions?" I ask.

"They are good for the local economy because of the income," Sherap says. "And for a time, there were many Everest expeditions."

"Because of *Into Thin Air* and the Imax film?"

"I think so. But now they are decreasing."

"The Maoists?"

At this, he shrugs. He doesn't want to talk about them. I had been surprised in Kathmandu by how many of my Nepalese friends had been supportive of the Maoists, and who had correctly predicted, some years ago, that they would be a force for the government to deal with. It astounded me that well-off Nepalese who were not the disenfranchised had expressed these opinions. This had nothing to do with supporting Communism, but their backing did have to do with the general dissatisfaction with the status quo and the rampant and widespread corruption of Nepalese politicians and government officials.

"What about the spiritual side of climbing Everest?" I ask now, diverting from the Maoist troubles. To know that so many people climb Everest, leaving dead bodies and oxygen bottles and rubbish diminishes the awe and sense of majesty that the mountain has for me.

"Everest is a goddess, but not really sacred," Sherap tells me. "For the Sherpa people, Khumbui Yul Lha is our sacred mountain."

On my map, it's directly above Namche.

"But it is only five thousand seven hundred metres high."

"No one has climbed Khumbui Yul Lha, and no one is allowed to climb this sacred mountain." Sherap laughs again, remembering a funny incident. I wait for him to continue. "In nineteen sixty-three, I saw toilet paper for the first time. I was ten years old. I hung it up on a wall because I thought it was a prayer flag."

I laugh with him. "And the changes you've seen since then are good?"

"More good than bad," he replies thoughtfully. " We have schools now, many sponsored by the Hillary Foundation. Before there were no schools, just monasteries."

The young Tamang girl comes into the room to feed dried yak dung into the flames of the space heater.

"Is that yak dung, or *zopkio* dung?" I ask Sherap.

He shrugs and replies, straight-faced. "Hard to tell the difference."

Stupid question.

As Sherap gets back to calculating his telephone bills, I write in my diary. Two attractive French-speaking women enter the dining room. One is blonde, the other dark-haired. They have both shared a hot shower and their hair is still wet. They sit by the space heater to let their hair dry. The blonde stands, conspicuously lowers her leggings down to her ankles, and then sits again. She applies moisturising cream on her naked thighs and calves. With her fleece top hanging over her lap, it's hard to tell if she has anything else on between the top and the leggings wrapped around her ankles. A Nepalese guide sitting on the other side of the space heater can scarcely contain himself as he watches the sensuous routine.

I order dinner from the menu by writing it down in a ledger book the size and shape of a Tibetan Buddhist prayer book. I suspect the dog-eared pages of this book are thumbed more often than the prayer books upstairs. The two women sit adjacent to me. We talk, in French. They ask the inevitable first question: *Vous montez, our vous descendez?* Are you going up or down? I learn that Genevieve and Caroline have just come down from the Gokyo Valley. They are both high from their trip and talkative.

"What was it like up there?" I ask.

"Beautiful," Genevieve, the blonde replies. She does most of the talking. "But cold. At night I could hardly sleep it was so cold."

Caroline, the dark one, is an occupational therapist. Her cousin Genevieve persuaded her to take a year off and travel.

"She's always travelling but this is my first trip," Carolyn says. "We'll start off together and then, well, we'll see…"

When I ask Genevieve what kind of work she does that she can travel all the time, she tells me that she's never worked in her life.

"You must do something," I insist.

"I used to be a tennis pro," she finally admits.

"That's work," I tell her.

They are both from Belgium, where Genevieve was relatively well known as a tennis player. Genevieve floats between travelling in the winter, spending time mysteriously in Thailand, and playing tennis in Europe during the summer. It hardly seems possible that she could be a professional tennis player. She seems so lithe, her legs too long, her shoulders too bony to be a pro. Her facial skin is as smooth as a baby's. Her top lip is slightly pointed and a little bubble appears at its tip when she speaks. Her bedroom eyes exude a benign sexuality.

We talk about Buddhism, meditation, retreats, work, careers, and life in general. They are unsure of their immediate plans after returning to Kathmandu.

"Are you going to Kala Pattar or Gokyo first?" Genevieve asks me.

"Kala Pattar," I reply.

"I'd like to do that." Genevieve looks at Caroline. "But Caroline has had enough, she wants to go back to Kathmandu, which she hasn't seen yet."

At eight, I take my leave, feeling the effects of the high altitude and the persistent cough and cold, which are wearing me down. The infrared sensors detect my movement and the lights go on as I head upstairs. I strip to my underwear, place my flip-flops beside my bed in case I have to get up in the middle of the night, and slide into my sleeping bag. I close my eyes and imagine the valley, as it must be now, encased in mist, perched over the gaping void. In the distance, I can hear the rhythmic metallic sound of yak bells and the random whine of a dog. Within seconds I am asleep.

5

Namche

When I awake the next morning, I sit up in bed and wipe the windowpanes free of the condensation that has accumulated during the night. I can see the mountaintops on the other side of the valley, bathed in orange light. Namche is still in the shadow of its basin.

My back is stiff and sore, and I'm only barely able to bend my back enough to reach my feet to get into my underpants and trousers, and then my socks and boots. I feel like an arthritic old man.

Several times during the night, I coughed up globules of bright yellow phlegm into a cushion of toilet paper. Now, in the morning light, little nests of paper litter the floor.

After a breakfast of milk coffee, a cheese and tomato omelette, and toast, I am refortified. I head down to the market, in the bowl-like fields immediately below the centre of Namche. The bright morning light slowly leaks down the hillside to where colourful Tibetans sit beside their Made-in-China wares, including fake Nike windproof jackets, North Face fleeces or down jackets, colourful Chinese fabrics, Nike shoes, Fubu jeans, thermoses, solar panel lights, dried sheep carcasses and animal hides. Some of the traders laugh when I take their photo, but others demand money. With their weathered skin and exotic looks, the Tibetans are photogenic. One holds up his coral-and-bead necklace around his neck, presumably offering the jewellery for sale.

"How much?" I ask him. *"Kati?"*

Speaking English or Nepali doesn't make any difference; he doesn't understand either. It is sign language, with the aid of a calculator, that is the *lingua franca* here.

When I show vague interest in the necklace, he pulls out a calculator and presses the keys to show me the price on the LCD. The numbers pop up: *300*. I pull out three hundred rupees and he laughs at me and shakes his head. He points at the figure on the calculator.

"Dollar," he tells me.

This time it is my turn to laugh. We laugh together, neither one of us fooled by the other. He wants three hundred dollars for it and I offered him three hundred rupees, not even the equivalent of five dollars. On the other hand, he wouldn't start with such an outrageous sum if there weren't those who were willing to pay close to what he was asking. No doubt some wealthy purchaser would go away bragging how he, or probably she, had bargained a Tibetan down to fifty dollars from three hundred dollars. The Tibetan would be just as delighted that he'd just earned a third of his annual income in five minutes.

I pass up on the offer of a necklace for three hundred dollars.

On three upper terraces, more conveniently located closer to the centre of Namche, is the Nepalese market, packed with sellers hawking fresh vegetables, fruit, boxes of dried goods, chocolate bars, porridge, Carlsberg beer, Pringle potato chips, utensils, Tiger Balm. Much of the dried goods have been carried by porter over a period of a more than a week from the trailhead at Jiri.

But now, at the end of the trekking season, with many flights flying in empty to pick up trekkers coming out, supplies are being flown in on the empty aircraft. Instead of trucking them all the way from Kathmandu to the trailhead at Jiri, and then transporting them on the backs of porters, they can be flown directly to Lukla, taken advantage of the unfilled aircraft.

I buy toilet paper for the trip, and a bag full of tangerines, and then sit in the warm sunlight at the Cyber Café in the centre of Namche. As I nibble on a chocolate-filled croissant, I recognise two of the trekking group I'd met in Lukla, sitting at the table next to me.

"Just arrived?" asks Bruce the Beard.

"Yesterday."

"Same as us," Bruce tells me. "We left after lunch the day we saw you in Lukla, and then we slept in Phakding before coming up here."

His wife studies me eating the *pain au chocolat* and asks, "Any good?"

"Delicious," I reply. It seems remarkable how we can find so much Western food way up here: pizzas, lasagnes, spaghetti bolognaise, French fries, cereal, porridge, and freshly brewed coffee. "Did you go to the market?" I ask.

"Yeah, but the locals just push and shove you around so we gave up," Bruce says.

"We're staying in lodges but the toilets are just shacks with holes in the ground. I hate having to squat like that," his wife says. "It's so bloody primitive. I don't see why they can't get proper toilets," she comments as an afterthought.

I feel myself being sucked into their bubble of negativity.

"Makes you realise what you've got back home," Bruce offers on a skewed positive note before getting up to make a telephone call, home to Australia.

His wife looks around the room.

"It's good to get away from the group," she says, as she finishes eating a croissant. "They're pretty uninspiring. I got sick in Kathmandu. Diarrhoea first and then vomiting. It's so bloody polluted there." She studies her ankle, bandaged in elastic tape. "Twisted my ankle in Lukla and then fell over and hit my head."

She's not having fun.

"Feel sorry for the yaks," she goes on. "They treat them pretty bad, beating them with sticks and throwing stones at them and everything."

Bruce the Beard returns to tell her everything is fine at home. But their litany of complaints about their trip continues to the point where I excuse myself and leave. If I don't, they'll have me stewing under the same black cloud.

I stroll up through the narrow alleys of Namche, up along the path beyond the Panorama Lodge to another lodge advertising *the highest hot tub in the world*. It's very tempting, but I continue on, up the steep ridgeline, stopping every few minutes to take a breath. The bird's-eye view over Namche, below, is worth the effort of the climb. At the top of the ridge I stroll easily over flat ground, past the Syangboche airstrip and then I climb, less steeply again, to the Everest View Hotel where oxygen tanks are kept in guests' rooms.

According to rumours I heard this morning in the bakery, there is a pressurised room for those trekkers, mostly Japanese, who have flown in to the Syangboche airstrip, and are suffering from altitude sickness. That's hardly surprising when they fly to an airstrip at almost four thousand metres, and then walk uphill to the hotel. Many of the afflicted have to be evacuated by helicopter.

This ramble up from Namche is another test of my back. Annabel didn't try to stop me from coming on this trip, far from it. But I had only just begun driving myself around in my car again and was only just able to sit upright when I left Bermuda. Walking long distances has always been my magical potion to overall mental and physical health. But these last few months it has proven to be more than a universal remedy. There is no doubt that walking has allowed me to make a remarkably fast recovery. Swimming every day helped too. Doctors told me that it would take a year to recover, if I was lucky. There were many days when I thought I'd broken my back again from overdoing my regimen of daily exercise. But five months after I'd shattered the L-2 vertebra into small pieces, I'm walking up to Everest Base Camp.

The Everest View Hotel is in a spectacular setting. Past the lip of the bowl overlooking Namche, set amongst pine trees and at the edge of open yak pastures, the hotel has a view up the valley towards Everest. From its vantage point I am perched incredibly high above the Imja Khola, which roars somewhere far below. The drop is so precipitous that my head reels and I feel such a dizziness that I fear I might inadvertently step over the edge into the abyss. I know immediately that I have vertigo. Moving about will only make it worse, so I sit on a rock for a few minutes until the sensation passes.

Recovered once again, I follow two members of the American group I had briefly met in the Kailash Lodge in Monjo. They are easily recognizable in their new high-tech extreme weather gear. One of them, not to be intimidated by his surroundings, pulls out a miniature but high-powered walkie-talkie.

"Papa Bear to Teddy Bear, how do you read over?"

No answer.

"Papa Bear to anyone, are you there? Over?"

His companion steps closer and stares down at the radio. 'Are you sure you put the batteries in it?" he asks.

The radio operator glances at me, a furtive, embarrassed look, before he puts the radio away. I try not to think of someone named Teddy Bear wandering aimlessly along the paths below. We all proceed to the terrace on the other side of the lobby where four Japanese sit at an outdoor table. The women lounge beneath wide-brimmed shade hats, listening to I-Pods while their husbands are busy with a smaller-than-a-laptop computer. One is tapping the keys while the other takes photos with a digital camera hooked up to the miniature laptop. Now and then they each take turns typing in messages, which I presume they will send on the hotel Internet service, unless their own unit is capable of being hooked up directly to an overhead satellite.

As I sit at a nearby table, a profusion of birds flit amongst the pines. In the distance Everest is shrouded in clouds. I try to imagine people climbing up there. What did Greg Hall, the mountain guide, brag? Anyone who could walk the streets of Kathmandu can be led to the summit of Everest. When Hillary and Tensing reached the summit of the mountain in 1951, it was one of the last great frontiers crossed by mankind, making headline news around the world. It seems a shame that the mountain should be sullied by such crass mountaineering commercialism, trivialising those first climbers' achievement in ascending the highest point on earth.

The late afternoon mist infiltrates, its fingers poking over the rim of the valley. I set off for Namche before it becomes so thick I cannot find my way back. In front of me a mountain floats discombobulated in the sky, impossibly high above. The two Americans stop by the path. They have a hand-held GPS, Global Positioning System, to confirm they are on the right route. Beyond them, and unnoticed by them, I see a group of animals that, at first, I think are goats. Then I see the massive male with his thick, dark coat and hunched shoulders and realize they are Himalayan thar, a strange looking animal, a cross between a goat and an ibex. The thar is a prehistoric relic, an animal capable of surviving in one of the remotest corners of the earth. I am surprised they are so close to Namche. It is not easy to make them out, but it is the first sign of wildlife I have seen.

I take my time returning to Namche, savouring being back in the Himalayas. It is good being here, wandering around aimlessly on my own for hours, lost in my thoughts, which inevitably keep returning to my brother, Kevin. When my father was a foreign correspondent in India and Kevin and I were at boarding school together in Delhi, we spent six weeks one summer holiday with my father in the Himalayas, in Kashmir, while my mother returned to Europe with my two sisters, one of whom had been quite sick. It was my first time in the Himalayas and the memories of horse riding, the house boats, fishing for trout in mountain streams are as sharp and clear as the air. I wonder how Kevin would enjoy being back in these same mountains. He never came back while I have returned now some fifteen or more times, mostly during that stint when I was monitoring the Canadian-funded aid projects. A feeling of sadness that Kevin and I never shared that early boyhood adventure again in the Himalayas overwhelms my buoyant spirits.

By the time I return to the ridge overlooking Namche, congealing clouds have almost hidden the village. From this perspective and with the illusion of the mist disguising the foreground, it looks as if I could take a running leap and land in the centre of the hamlet. I take my time walking back and arrive at the Panorama Lodge cold and hungry where I ask for a tomato soup from the smiling Tamang girl. A Sherpa, semi-reclined on the Tibetan carpet covering the bench seats, head propped up on the palm of one crooked elbow, eyes me carefully. I can tell he is eager to talk.

"I've travelled all over the United States, in almost every state," he says finally. "I go there every year. My American friend is a doctor and his wife is a lawyer. They have five houses and each house has five bedrooms and each bedroom has a toilet."

I eat my soup and listen politely as he tells me all the places he has been in America. He has travelled more than most Americans have in their own country. Abruptly, he sits up to massage his toes.

"My feet hurt from the walk up here," he says.

"From Lukla?"

"Yes." He puts on a jacket emblazoned with a list of the world's seven highest summits before he exits to find his South African clients.

I return to my room and change out of clothes soaked in perspiration and replace them with a dry set. Reluctant to put on my heavy boots, I pull on a pair of woollen socks and a pair of sandals and set off down into Namche. In the middle of the narrow streets I bump into Yes Yes Shelly, a woman I met in Kathmandu at the airport while waiting for our flight to Lukla. She was full of enthusiasm for her trek to Everest Base Camp, and for her guide.

"You look lost," I tell her.

"No, no, I'm looking for Sonam, my guide," she says. "I gave him some money to buy a down jacket but I haven't seen him since. He said he'd just be a few minutes and we'd meet here in front of the bakery."

"You bought him a down jacket?" I ask.

"Yes, yes. He must be warm for our trip." She looks around, worried.

"I hope he hasn't taken off."

"Maybe we can check the Paradise Club," she thinks aloud. "He took me there last night."

We wander through Namche to the Paradise Club and walk up the staircase to a dark room decorated with yak skins and mummified yak skulls. Beside the bar is a television showing a Bruce Lee video. A dozen Sherpa guides stare, transfixed by Bruce Lee's invincibility. They grunt and groan in unison with each punch Bruce throws, each kick he makes. Shelly stalks around the smoky room in search of her guide. There are some Westerners in the bar, but they are in the minority. Apart from the mummified yak heads on the walls, the bar seems outlandishly out of place in this high mountain setting. It reminds me of the bizarre Galactic Bar in the Star Wars films, a room full of weird-looking characters peering through the smoke and half-light. Several of these otherworldly denizens play pool at a table that must have taken half-a-dozen porters weeks to carry up from the road. It wouldn't surprise me if this was the highest game of pool being played anywhere on earth.

I study the price list of drinks, listed in coloured chalk on a blackboard above the bar. Even by Western standards, the prices are not cheap. I wonder how the Sherpas can afford to drink here, much less get drunk, as some of them clearly are. When Shelly returns, without her missing guide, I point out to her the high prices of the drinks.

"No, no," she says, "Those are the prices for Westerners. The Sherpas get it for half price. I gave Sonam the money and he bought the drinks for us much cheaper. Yes, yes. Even the bakery prices are different, although they only advertise the prices for Westerners."

We go into the *Pizza Hut* bar where young Sherpas play pool and Western music blares from tinny speakers.

"I'll be a moment," I tell Shelly. "I want to check out this sign advertising a sauna."

The bartender yells for someone to take me to the sauna. He opens a heavy wooden door to a proper Scandinavian-type sauna with wooden walls, ceiling, benches and round river stones over an electric heater to give off steam.

"Four hundred rupees, no time limit," he tells me. "Showers over there, as many you want. Also a laundry service while you have a sauna so everything is clean when you finish. Seven dollars." That's not bad when you really want one, although it would be a small fortune for the average Nepalese.

Shelly gives up looking for Sonam and we head over to the bakery for a hot chocolate and a donut.

"I don't know where he is," she tells me as we climb flagstone steps. "He said he'd meet me in the bar. Anyway, it's good that he is on his own for a bit. We've been together the whole time since Kathmandu." She looks a bit heartbroken as she says this. "Yes, yes," she adds, as if to persuade herself that she's right about it being good for Sonam to spend some time on his own. Then, as if forcing her mind off her AWOL guide, she says, "I spoke to the headmaster of the school in Lukla. They want me to stay for a year and teach English there."

The bakery is the prime meeting point in Namche, where one can get all the local scuttlebutt. The Belgian girls, Genevieve and Caroline are there, talking to two beaming men. Shelly and I buy our hot chocolates and chocolate donuts and sit down at their table. Genevieve makes the introductions.

"Mark, this is Andrew," she says. "Andrew's staying at the same lodge as us."

Mark gets up unexpectedly and goes to sit next to a woman who is reading, alone, at another table. She is slim and rather beautiful. I guess by her looks that she is a Nepali. Since Mark does not say anything as he sits next to her, I assume they are a couple. Now Caroline introduces me to Ben, the other man at the table.

He has a wide grin permanently pasted to his face. We shake hands and I introduce them to Shelly.

"Yes, yes," Shelly says, when asked if she is going trekking. "I am going up the Gokyo Valley and then the Everest Valley. I'm going to spend some days at the Tengboche Monastery."

"Tengboche reminds me of Disney World," Ben tells her, speaking with apparent authority. "It's lit up by floodlights at night, they have a souvenir shop selling postcards and Tengboche T-shirts and it's run by a Westerner. A German named Michael. From what my guides tell me, he takes a cut of all the earnings."

"Yes, yes, well, I want to go and spend some time with the lama there," Shelly replies, oblivious to his comments. "I bumped into the lama on the path up to Namche and he said he knew I was coming to see him. It was incredible. He just knew it. Yes, yes. He invited me to stay for a week." Although she is from Western Canada, she has a peculiar accent, as if she learned English as a second language. Maybe it's because she's been talking like this for Sonam, and doesn't know how to switch it off.

"Ben has just climbed Island Peak," Genevieve says.

"Was it difficult?" I ask wide-eyed.

"It was okay," Ben says. He is nonchalant.

"Did you use ropes?" I am genuinely interested. Island Peak, known locally as

Imja Tse, is a 6000-metre peak and one of the most popular for climbing and trekking. From Dingboche, the mountain appears as a pyramid of rock and ice. But it provides some of the most awe-inspiring scenery in the Khumbu region. I've considered climbing Island Peak myself, but I've never really been sure how technically difficult it is.

"No ropes," Ben replies. "And that surprised me because some of the drops were steep, especially near the top."

'You went on your own?"

"I'm the only client, but I have a staff of nine looking after me. *Sirdars*, guides, porters, cooks, and kitchen boys. You name it. I don't have to do a thing." He laughs and a smile spreads across his face again. "I hear you're a writer."

"I've really just started," I say.

"Ever heard of John Berger? I really enjoy his work. How about..." He names more writers I don't know. I feel illiterate. He hands me *To the Wedding*, a novel by Berger. "I've finished it, you can borrow it."

"I'm not likely to be able to finish it before I leave Namche."

"Keep it," he insists.

"Ben's a doctor," Genevieve tells me, ever amenable to extolling the virtues of others.

"Really? What kind?" I ask.

"Oh, just a surgeon," Ben replies.

"*Just* a surgeon," Genevieve repeats with irony.

Now Genevieve and Caroline speak French to each other and this annoys Ben who can't understand what they are saying. They get up and disappear out the back, ostensibly for the toilets. But I notice a look of collusion on their faces.

"I saw Genevieve and Caroline further up the trail," Ben tells me. "I was hoping I might meet them here." His grin seems glued permanently to his face.

"Where are you staying?" I ask.

"In a tent with my staff."

"Why don't you come up to our lodge tonight for dinner," I invite.

He shakes his head. "My cook has already taken my order for dinner."

"Then come up for a drink."

"Good idea."

I like Ben. It would be nice to meet up with him later this evening. Genevieve and Caroline come back from wherever they were. I get up to leave, knowing the two women will persuade Ben to come over to our lodge for a drink. I say goodbye to Mark at the adjacent table, but he ignores me. He has sidled up to the pretty Asian sitting next to him. I'm befuddled by the group dynamics here. And although I am usually an acute observer of human nature, I'm also sometimes incredibly naïve.

Yes Yes Shelly decides to continue ferreting out Sonam, her erstwhile guide, who should be wearing a new down jacket if he hasn't run off with her money. "See you up in the mountains," I tell her.

"Yes, yes," she replies, and steps out into the mist swirling through Namche.

A line of yaks returning to Tibet with sacks of rice meander through the village and up the path ascending past my lodge. The heavy bronze bells dangling under their necks seem to ring even louder in the mist, perhaps because my auditory senses are more acute when there is nothing to see. The men, some of whom are so sunburned their faces seem purple, "*chuui*" the yak along, occasionally raising their arms as if to throw a stone. Their progress is slow but steady as they transport goods from Namche over the high mountain passes to trade back in Tibet.

In the warm dining room of the Panorama Lodge, several other trekkers wait for their dinners. They are all ages, although it surprises me how old some of them are. A young man swaggers in with several others in tow. He loudly claims to be a mountaineer and a mountain guide back home in Oregon, taking climbers up mountains. Although he talks to his own entourage of friends whom he met up here, his voice carries so that all of us in the dining room can hear him. He wants to expand his business to Nepal and is looking for a Nepalese partner.

"Problem is," he says, "Everyone is here trying to find a Sherpa partner to work with."

Ten more trekkers walk into the room. Unlike the would-be climber looking for a Sherpa partner, these trekkers are all Those Going Down. They are burned by sun and wind. Visibly exhausted, they drop their high-tech, spring-loaded walking sticks in a pile in the corner and remove their jackets and day backs. A lonely trekker occupies one side of the room and they ask him to move, giving them a place. Their guide follows. Almost two metres tall, I imagine him to be a bona fide mountaineer with his straggly long hair pulled back in a ponytail. His beard is unkempt, his hands are huge, his fingers scarred, probably from rock falls. He is muscular and lean, with deep-set eyes. His clients are noticeably quiet as he pulls out a plastic chair. He has that wild, Reinhold Messner look about him. Unlike the young braggart in the opposite corner with the loud voice, this mountaineer doesn't speak. He doesn't need to. His presence is commanding enough. By comparison the braggart looks like a toddler learning to walk. The group settles back into their seats as the little Tamang girl takes their drinks orders.

Genevieve and Caroline join me for dinner. As we did the night before, we talk at length about many subjects. I enjoy their company. The tall guide casts his deep-set eyes in our direction, presumably hoping to make eye contact with Genevieve or Caroline.

"Did you tell Ben you have a girlfriend back home?" Caroline asks.

"Yes," I reply, truthfully. "What about you?"

She shakes her head. "I haven't had a boyfriend for two years."

"And you?" I look at Genevieve.

She hesitates at first, and then says, "I have a boyfriend, yes."

"Where?"

"He lives in Thailand, when he is not looking after his mother in Italy."

That accounts for her mysterious trips there. "What's he doing in Thailand?"

"He meditates," she replies.

"All day?"

"All the time."

"How's he live? I mean, what does he do for a living so he can afford to eat?"

Caroline studies Genevieve, waiting for her answer.

"He does nothing. He's a hermit."

"Really?" I look at Caroline for confirmation.

"When I saw him for the first time I couldn't imagine him with Genevieve," she says. Then quickly adds, "I don't mean to offend you, Genevieve."

"Have you been going out with him for long?" I ask.

"Two years."

"How often do you see him?"

"Every couple of months, unless it's the summer, when I play tennis."

"But that can't be good for him. I mean, he's living like an ascetic and then, suddenly, bam! You arrive."

I look at her, and remember her rubbing the cream into her long lithe legs. I imagine this man, living alone in a cave for several months, and then Genevieve shows up with her long legs and cream in her purse.

"How long do you get together?"

"A couple of days, or weeks."

"And then it's back to contemplating his own navel for some months until you come back again?" I ask. "That's not really a relationship."

"Well, what about you?" she asks. "You have a girlfriend, but you are here on your own. What are you doing here?"

It's not an aggressive question so much as an inquisitive one, so I think about what she has asked me.

"I'll tell you why I'm here alone," I say. "And I think if I tell you in French, I will be able to tell you without crying."

"*Oui…?*" Caroline says, encouraging me. So, in French, I tell her about Kevin dying alone in that Texas hotel. About my accident six weeks later. About the envelope I am carrying with me containing the few strands of my brother's hair. Speaking in another language helps distance me from my emotions.

The loud Oregon mountain climber makes a big deal about pumping water out of a bucket into a water bottle. He could use iodine tablets instead, which would be so much easier than pumping water through a water-filter. But it wouldn't be as noticeable, and it's obvious he wants to be noticed at every turn.

"I'm sorry," Carline says. She looks like I feel.

"It's been a difficult year," I tell her. "Annabel couldn't take time off work to come with me, but I needed the time to be alone anyway." I let out a big breath of air. Done. It was easier to tell Caroline now than it was Suzanne in Kathmandu, just a week ago.

Ben joins us, still unwashed since his expedition up Island Peak, still sporting a wicked trekker's head, with greasy matted hair sticking up in all directions. He carries it off well and the permanent smile in the middle of his sunburned face is sufficient distraction. The lodge is packed and as we talk the other guests head to the rooms. Even the Nepalese guides and porters sitting around the space heater have started to thin out. I, too, am tired from the walk up to the Everest View Hotel, and unlike the other three, still not acclimatised. I say goodnight and then leave to snuggle into my warm sleeping bag. But on the way through to the kitchen, Sherap tells me that every Saturday night he and his wife meet at Lhakpa's mother's for buffalo momo dinner. He asks me if

I want to join them. It's too good an opportunity to miss, despite my fatigue.

We walk outside using flashlights to light the path. The mist has gone and the air is cold, the sky black and clear and studded with stars. At another lodge, at the same contour level as the Panorama, we enter a building under construction. In a corner of what will become the dining room is a small portable iron stove with red-hot embers glowing inside. The extended Sherpa family sits huddled around the fire. They welcome me to the group and I am introduced to Lhakpa's relatives. The mother is a strong-faced woman, not that much older than Lhakpa. Her three sisters are there too, and her youngest brother. In a far corner of the room is a television showing a satellite programme from Indian Star television. I am offered clear *rakshi*, a rice wine, and within minutes, plates of steaming buffalo momo soup are served to each of us. A dish of hot chilli is passed around. The soup is delicious.

I can often feel more comfortable in rustic settings such as this, mixing with villagers. My ability to relate to locals is no doubt directly connected to the long periods I have spent in Africa and Asia as a child, followed by those years living in the bush in Africa and several years doing development work in isolated villages throughout the two continents. I feel more at ease in these settings than my own Western environment. Western materialism has never tempted me while these voluntary excursions into Third World poverty feel more natural. Of course I can always extract myself from these circumstances and yet I often daydream about spending indefinite periods in these settings again.

Like many Westerners who spend long periods in rural Asia, Africa and South America, I find it easier to adapt to the slower, less stressful pace of a rural village in the middle of nowhere than the re-entry back into my own world.

My hosts talk in dialect but each of them politely takes a turn to engage me in conversation at some point in the evening. To my right is a shopkeeper I recognise from the Bazaar. I bought batteries for my camera from him. I ask if those were real Patagonia and North Face clothes he had in his store.

"Every summer I go to New England to buy clothes directly from the manufacturer," he tells me. Like Sherap, his English is almost perfect. "I import them here. It is still cheaper than you can buy for retail in the United States."

Conversation stops whenever there is an action sequence on the Indian video, which must have been filmed in Switzerland or somewhere in Europe. A Jeep full of singing Indian actors, collectively gyrating their hips, careens down verdant country lanes before the speeding vehicle enters a neat European town with streetcars. Strange, watching an Indian video filmed in Europe while eating buffalo momos, huddled around an open brazier for warmth, and drinking *rakshi* in the middle of the Himalayas.

A swarm of children enters the room. They have just returned from a birthday party and are dressed in party mode, their faces spotlessly clean, their hair neatly combed. Each child clutches a little 'goodie' bag given by the parents of the birthday child. In the bags are paper hats, those whistles you blow that uncoil like snakes, and other spoils. They proudly show their parents what they have, then sit on a bed in the corner of the room and watch the television with the rest of us. Most of the children are so exhausted they fall asleep within minutes.

"Chombi, who runs Kailash Lodge in Monjo, told me that almost any Sherpa could climb to the top of Everest," I tell Sherap. "Do you think that is true?"

Sherap twists the hairs at the corner of his sparse moustache and thinks about the question before he replies.

"I think that is true," he says, and laughs. "Especially if, like the Western climbers, the Sherpas had porters climbing ahead to establish base camps with tents ready, and hot food waiting and thermoses of hot tea, and tanks of oxygen. I think most Sherpas could climb Everest in such case." He laughs again and tells the others in his own dialect what we have been talking about. They laugh too, agreeing with him.

It's a wonderfully hospitable evening, a blending of old-fashioned Sherpa culture and hospitality with the increasing influence of Western society and values. I have only been in the Khumbu for a couple of days and already I am surprised by the extent to which the Sherpas have adapted to the influence of the Western world. I thank my hosts for the evening and then, allowing my eyes to adjust to the darkness rather than use my flashlight, I walk slowly back to the Panorama Lodge. It is very cold, but it is a dry cold, and the sky is perfectly clear with an almost full moon bathing Namche in its silvery light. The surrounding mountains are ghostly apparitions, silent, powerful. I stand looking at them until my feet are too cold to remain outside any longer.

6

Side Trip to Thame

At breakfast Caroline and Genevieve tell me they have decided to accompany me to Thame for the day. I had told them about my plans to make this side trip further up the valley to give me another day of altitude acclimatisation, as well as another day to get my back into shape before heading up to Everest Base Camp. Too often I have walked in the mountains, especially here in Nepal, on my own. Their company will be a welcome change. They ask me if I mind if Ben joins us. Despite wanting to come here to think, I'll have plenty of time over the next three weeks to walk in solitude.

We wait in the dining room of the lodge for Ben, who shows up with the pretty Asian girl from the bakery. He walks past me as if I was invisible and places his hands on Genevieve's arms. He stares intently into her eyes, his smile pasted to his face. He is in love. Or lust. Probably both.

Caroline comes out of the kitchen, her face showing displeasure.

"We've been asked to move out of our lodge," she tells us quietly. "They're fully booked tonight so Lhakpa's booked us in to her sister's lodge."

"What happened last night?" I ask.

"We were here until late," Ben replies. "Caroline went to bed and Genevieve and I just talked here in the dining room. I felt like Cyrano de Bergerac, though, when I had to climb over the walls to get out. They'd locked the gate."

Lhakpa's had enough bad experiences with trekkers and their amorous ways to nip trouble in the bud before it happens.

"Put your packs in my room," I offer. I'm eager to begin the day and don't relish waiting for them to move their belongings to the other lodge. "You can move later. Otherwise it'll take forever and the day will be gone."

Ben introduces me to the pretty Asian-looking woman, whose name is Laxmi, and who is, in fact, an American and another surgeon from the States. They met in the bakery yesterday, with Mark. She will join us too on the side trip to Thame.

Finally we set off, skirting Namche, walking along a perimeter path contouring around the lip, rather than down into the bowl and back up again. Soon after cresting the ridge overlooking Namche, we are in forest. I hang back from the others, relishing the peacefulness of this perfect morning with clear blue skies and a pine woods resonating with birdsong. I walk slowly and soon their voices are out of earshot. Then I hear new voices, this time from behind. I try to stay ahead of the intrusive voices, caught between the others in front and the group behind. Every time I stop to listen to the birds, or the trickling of water down a creek crossing the path, or the sound of bells of yaks or *zopkios*, the group behind catches up enough that I hear them talking in excited tones. Eventually I stop and let the group pass me. They walk in a tight bunch, chatting away.

At a small creek with a *kani*, a walk-through stone structure that marks the entrance to a village, I see several danphe, the national bird of Nepal. The birds are unafraid, providing me with a detailed look at their colourful plumage. More than anything else, they look like multi-coloured peacocks, but without the benefit of enormous tail feathers. At Pare village I catch up to the others sitting on the open terrace of a lodge. The sun is strong and we are soon warm, basking in its light. I listen vaguely, while watching Alpine choughs play in the currents of wind. The other group walks by in a tight clump, still chattering away. The older woman, who is their guide, is apparently lost and leads them around the village, in search of something. A few minutes later they file into the dark interior of a lodge to have lunch. It's as if they have disappeared into a vacuum.

The views are spectacular and we sit there relaxing for half an hour before continuing on to Thame. Laxmi walks beside me.

"I didn't sleep well last night,' she tells me. "Mark the Flake was bothering me."

"Mark the Flake?" I struggle with the weight of my daypack and twinges of pain along my spine that I haven't felt before.

"The guy sitting in the bakery when you walked in," Laxmi says. "Everyone in Namche calls him 'Mark the Flake'. He knocked on the door of my dormitory last night and asked me if I wanted a massage. I was all alone in there. It was already ten o'clock and I'd been asleep for a couple of hours. I told him I no, but he moved into the dormitory anyway and slept in one of the other beds. I couldn't sleep all night."

"I thought the two of you were together when I saw you sitting side by side in the bakery," I say.

"Oh no," Laxmi replies. "I had just arrived in Namche that morning. I went in to the bakery before I had even found a lodge. Mark was talking loudly about how he had been the doctor for a climbing expedition to Island Peak. He goes on and on about the climbing expedition to anyone in the bakery. He asked me if I wanted to see his patients. I mean, both of us being doctors, I trusted him. And I was interested in seeing what kind of medical problems there are in Namche. He told me he was the Namche doctor but he isn't the Namche doctor at all. He's just another trekker like us, with a lot of time on his hands, which I don't understand. I mean, how does he get so much time off like this to hang around a bakery in the Himalayas? It's not like he's my age."

As she talks, I swing my walking stick under my pack and grab it with my other hand and let the pack rest on it to take some of the weight off my back. As it turned out, Mark the Flake had shown Laxmi some patients in Namche but there was nothing more than blisters, diarrhoea. Thinking the lodge where he was staying looked fine, she had taken a bed in the dormitory, which was empty. He had left her there and went back down to the bakery while she unpacked. It was later that afternoon, when Laxmi came to the bakery herself that she found him talking in French to Genevieve and Caroline. Apparently, he had turned his attention from her to the Belgian women, until I came in and interrupted them.

"He keeps telling everyone that he speaks four languages," she adds. "He's definitely got a problem. From what I hear, he just hangs around Namche trying to pick up girls half his age. He's in his forties and has a kid in high school. He was about to go down to Lukla but changed his mind when I told him I was going to Gokyo. He says he might go up there too. I don't want him stalking me. Are you going to Gokyo?"

"After Everest Base Camp," I say.

As we walk, I learn more about Laxmi. Her father is from Goa. He immigrated to the States and met her mother, who is from the Philippines. Now I understand why she looks Nepalese. She's been travelling for six months. She took the time off after working in South Africa, before she moves back to the States.

"I was supposed to be getting married this month," she says suddenly. "My boyfriend asked me to get married in March. In April, he decided to climb Mt. McKinley and didn't ask me what I thought. We've been going out since I was eighteen. We both like climbing. When we first met, part of the attraction was that he was a climber, but now I realise he'll always be taking time to climb, risking his life. It's that ego thing. It's okay when you're young, but he's in his thirties now and it's not so appealing to me any more. I broke off our engagement."

She steps across a narrow stream crossing the path. As I follow her, I again shift more of the backpack's weight onto the stick that I hold firmly in my hands. At least her incessant talk about herself helps me ignore my own mental can of worms. She tells me that while her parents are happy with their own lives, they are not happy with their daughter's life. Although her boyfriend is a surgeon, he also happens to be a black surgeon. Her parents have hardly spoken to her since she's been dating him.

"But your own parents are a mixed marriage," I note.

"I don't get it either," she says. "I guess they're just racist. Anyway, they're happy now that we've split up."

She continues talking about herself until we reach the outskirts of the village of Thame where the others are waiting for us. Caroline is the first to speak. "How's your back, Andrew?"

"Not so good," I tell her honestly. It's hardly surprising. The day I left the hospital, the radiologist who had been on duty when the ambulance brought me in asked if I wanted to see my CAT-Scans. I went into his office and there were the backlit negatives, on the wall. He pointed out the damage. "I was just showing these to another doctor. You look at these detailed images of a spine with a burst vertebra and you would think the patient would without question have been paralysed. You've very lucky to be walking out of here after that kind of massive injury to your back."

Ben doesn't have a pack, not even a daypack. His expedition cook, Ganesh, has accompanied us to make sure that Ben doesn't get hungry. And he has carried Ben's daypack for him.

"Let me take you pack," Ben offers gallantly.

I unload my daypack stuffed full of camera and lenses and some extra clothes. The pack must weigh five or six kilos. I hand it over to Ben, and thank him as he falls in step beside me. As we walk together now, I ask him if he has a girlfriend waiting back home.

"Uh uh. Have to fight them off," Ben says before he outpaces me in order to catch up to Genevieve. I smile. He might fight them off back home, I think to myself, but he's certainly adopted a different strategy in the Himalayas.

Half an hour later, we walk into Thame, a quiet village with a stream trickling through it, flat yak pasture enclosures, and friendly Sherpa people. Because it is not on the direct route to Everest or Gokyo Lakes, it's the most authentic looking Sherpa village I've seen yet. Those Westerners who come here have to take a detour to get to this village. We settle against a wall and bask in the strong sunlight. We don't even have to go into the lodge to order our food as Ben's personal expedition cook, Ganesh, brings the menus to us.

The backache I felt the first two days has returned. I worry it is more than just soft tissue seizing up, that maybe it's a damaged disc objecting to the increased pressure placed on it. Genevieve sees me moving stiffly as I sit down.

"Want a massage?" she asks. She had told me that first night how she'd like to give up tennis, and start a small get-well centre, with health food and a massage therapist.

She gives me her fleece jacket to lie on and I flop down on top of the wall as she rubs my back. Ben mutters something about his back being sore, too. Genevieve keeps up the massage until lunch is ready and then we join the others. We sprawl at the edge of a warm patch of grass. Ben can hardly keep his hands off Genevieve as she sits astride him, facing him. Ganesh, the cook, hands out our lunch: soup and French-fries. Then he stands to the side of the group, eyeing his client. He knows Ben has only recently met Genevieve. For a woman to be so blatantly sexual after just meeting his client is mind-boggling to the Nepali. Her leggings show off her long athletic legs and provoke the senses. The rest of us try to ignore the sizzling relationship.

Jesus Rays poke through puffy clouds high above, a reminder that we should head back to Namche before the afternoon mist comes up the valley. When Laxmi asks for her plastic bottle to be refilled with water, Ganesh takes it and returns the bottle.

"This is hot water," Laxmi tells him. "I wanted cold water. They charge for boiled water." She hands the bottle back to Ganesh. There's an awkward silence. Ganesh doesn't know what to do as he stands there with the bottle in his hand.

"I'll pay for it," Ben says impatiently. "It's only sixty rupees." The uncomfortable situation is diffused. Since Ben has paid thousands of dollars to summit Island Peak with a personal entourage of nine, sixty rupees is nothing for him. But for Laxmi, apparently, it was something to quibble about. No wonder the lodge owners prefer the expedition clients.

Wanting to see the village *gompa*, I head in the direction of a ridge to take a quick look. The others soon yell up to me, and signal that they are going back down to Namche. I turn around and reluctantly follow suit. Recovering from a broken back, it's not such a good idea to go off exploring on my own, with a long walk ahead. Unlike the others, who are all acclimatised to the altitude, Laxmi suffers from a headache again as we head down. Ben has taken my backpack and is off like a sheepdog, dancing around Genevieve.

"Two days ago," Laxmi tells me, "I met a climber. He talked my ears off for two and a half hours about climbing Ama Dablam. He described the different snow and ice conditions, the relative advantages of the crampons he uses, and the technical difficulty of the different pitches on the mountain. Lots of things. But he was so long-winded and boring I had to excuse myself and leave. Climbers are like that. They go on and on and on about the climbs they've done. No wonder there's so many books about climbing."

As we descend the path back down to Namche, she gets herself really worked up about the general flakiness of men. "I've never met so many guys wandering around aimlessly trying to figure out their lives as I have here in Nepal," she notes. "You should hear some of the bullshit I've heard. You can't believe anything they tell you."

At a dip in the path I bump into Caroline resting by a *mani* wall. She is quieter than Laxmi, not such a compulsive talker and for me, an easier companion to walk and be with. Although she doesn't say much, Caroline takes it all in. This is her first time travelling outside of Europe. The three of us set off together but I continue with Caroline, letting Laxmi go on her own.

"Are you sure Laxmi is okay by herself?" Caroline asks, concerned.

"She's fine. She needs some time by herself."

By contrast, Caroline and I walk in comfortable silence. On several occasions we come across groups of daphne, almost always in pairs. The males are iridescent fat things while the females are a plainer brown and white. Twice we see small groups of Himalayan thar. They seem to be impervious to our presence as they scramble amongst steep rocky cliffs. With the lack of conversation I become more aware of the ambient sounds, the trickling water of streams, the sound of the yak bells, the numerous birds singing, the dull roar of the river far below. Occasionally there is a whistling sound as several alpine choughs descend, their wings folded back like miniature jet fighters. A flock of snow pigeons twists and turns in compact formation flying.

The sun has set behind the high mountains to the east and already we are in shadow and it is starting to get dark. We round a spur dominated by boulders carved with Tibetan prayers and suddenly find Namche below, nestled in its cradle-like bowl. The full moon rises above Thamserku. I stop at the unexpected sight of the settlement bathed in the bright moonlight. We watch the full moon rising in the ambient stillness. It's an awesome sight. Neither of us says anything for several minutes. Prayer flags hoisted on bamboo poles atop carved boulders flutter lightly in the breeze. The moonlight is so intense that the colours on the prayer flags show up clearly. It might as well be daylight. In the valley below, the congealed mist is silvery where the slanted light of the moon touches, purple where the moonlight has not yet reached. Even Namche seems strangely quiet despite the warm lights of the lodges.

Thamserku, Ama Dablam and Kangtaiga are black silhouettes against the rising moon. Behind us, towards Thame, the mountains are startling white in the silvery moonlight.

We contour down, past the *gompa* and around the perimeter of the bowl back to the Panorama Lodge. Genevieve and Ben are not there. Hungry from the day's walk, Caroline and I order soup and a thermos of lemon tea from the kitchen. The lodge is full, with large trekking groups.

"Ben wants Genevieve to come to Seattle and live with him," Caroline tells me. " He's proposed marriage."

"But they've only just met!" I reply, unable to contain my surprise.

"She's supposed to be going out with an Italian ascetic in Thailand who flies back home occasionally to look after his mother and now she's going to marry a brain surgeon in America." Caroline shrugs as she takes up her cup of lemon tea.

"He's not a brain surgeon," I say, even though I know it's quibbling.

"Whatever."

"Do you think it will work?"

"I don't know," Caroline says. "Genevieve admits it's easy to fall in love in the mountains, the special atmosphere here amongst travellers. She can't sleep at night. She talks about him all the time, but she's scared about what will happen in the future. What do you think will happen?"

"I think she'll go to America but I don't think she'll stay," I answer. "He'll be too controlling, and she's too much of a free spirit." It's my honest opinion.

Caroline and I wait for over an hour before Genevieve and Ben enter the dining room. They had been waiting for us down in the bakery.

"We saw Mark the Flake," Genevieve tells Caroline in French. I notice again that Ben is clearly uncomfortable around Caroline and Genevieve when they speak French together. "He walked out of the bakery as soon as he saw us walk in. Laxmi arrived later. She's decided to go up to Gokyo tomorrow."

It is crowded in the dining room and there is nowhere for Ben and Genevieve to sit. All the bench seats on the walls are taken and Nepalese guides sitting around the space heater occupy the plastic seats. Lhakpa comes out and confirms to Genevieve that there is no room for them in the Panorama tonight. Their bags remain upstairs in my room waiting to be taken to Lhakpa's sister's Moonlight Lodge.

Ben's *sirdar* comes in to the dining room with Ganesh the cook. Judging from the loudness of the *sirdar*'s voice, he has been drinking. An argument breaks out when Ben says flatly that he doesn't want to eat dinner alone with them in his dining tent. It's public and very loud and soon becomes embarrassing. Lhakpa hurries out of the kitchen, concerned at the ruckus in her lodge caused by these outsiders. All this time, Genevieve and Caroline have been discussing their options in French.

"Listen," I tell them, also in French, "why don't you get your packs and go to the other lodge where Lhakpa has booked you? Then, you can sort things out there."

Genevieve relays my suggestion to Ben, who has by now agreed with his *sirdar* and cook that he will come down to his tent for dinner. The two of them head for my room and Caroline and I wait for them to return with their packs. My back is still bothering me. I'm ready for a hot shower. And despite having had the bowl of soup, I'm hungry. I want to eat dinner soon and so does Caroline.

Twenty minutes pass and no Ben or Genevieve. Caroline goes up to the bedrooms and calls out their names. There is no response so she returns to the dining room. Another ten minutes of waiting and it's my turn to check on what's what. I find the key is still in the door of my room. I open it slowly. There are Genevieve and Ben, lying on my bed, her shirt pulled almost over her head, his hands caressing her naked body. They jump at the sight of me and Genevieve quickly pulls her shirt back down.

"It's not fair," I tell her in French. "Caroline doesn't know what's going on. I'm tired. I'd like a shower and dinner." I glance at Ben. "Be a pal Ben. Tie it in a knot until you get to their lodge." I say this quickly in English so that Genevieve might not understand.

Ben apologises so I go back downstairs where I begin to see the humour in the situation. When the two of them come into the dining room a few minutes later, they are apologetic and a bit rumpled. They invite me for dinner at their lodge.

"I'll have my dinner here," I tell them. "It's bad form to have dinner in another lodge, even if it *is* Lhakpa's sister's place. I'll be there in an hour."

An hour later, I'm refreshed. Clean, full of food, and dressed in warm dry clothes, I walk over to the Moonlight Lodge. I don't need a flashlight. The moonlight reveals every pebble on the dusty pathway. It is otherworldly walking in this bright moonlight through slumbering Namche Bazaar.

Caroline, Genevieve and Ben are in the dining lounge of their lodge. At first glance the lodge looks empty, but it is actually full. All the other clients have already left the lounge and gone to bed. Ben has the same perpetual smile creasing his face. He didn't make it down to his camp for dinner after all. There are no spare bedrooms left and Caroline and Genevieve have been assigned the prayer room, replete with a statue of the Buddha. I notice several porters, anxious to turn on the video. But the proprietor won't let them watch it as long as there are trekkers still in the dining room. Finally, the porters give up waiting for us to leave and pull out blankets to spread on the Tibetan carpets covering the bench seats. One removes his shoes and the smell is so overpowering I have to excuse myself.

"I should head back now," I tell the others. "It's getting late. You're all leaving tomorrow?"

Caroline and Genevieve look at each other. They still haven't decided what they are doing.

"See you at the bakery in the morning?" Caroline asks me. "At nine?"

"Sure."

I'm only going as far as Khunde, so I don't have to leave early. When I walk back to the Panorama Lodge. It's even quieter than before. There are no clouds and the moon is up so high its light shines on the western flanks of Thamserku and Ama Dablam. The mountains all around are bathed in the sharp moonlight. It's a sight that stirs my senses, and a wave of loneliness overtakes me as my thoughts turn inevitably to Kevin.

As youngsters, living in Africa and Asia, Kevin and I shared a room and often the same bed. He had a habit of sleepwalking, but we were told never to wake him. In Hong Kong, he often knocked on the cook's door to wake him. Even in his sleep, Kevin wanted

Ah Wong to play cards. The cook was also under strict instructions never to disturb Kevin when he was sleepwalking. As a result, an exhausted Ah Wong spent hours playing Snap on the back doorsteps of our house, in the middle of the night, with a boy who was sound asleep.

I stand outside for almost an hour to absorb the impressions so that I can better remember the experience.

7

Khunde Hospital

I wake up coughing. The top of my sleeping bag is wet with condensation again. I wipe the water off the inside of the windowpanes and peer out. The dawn illuminates the tips of the mountains with its bright orange light. I get out of bed and dress quickly in the cold.

In the dining room, Rema, the Tamang girl with the lovely smile, takes my breakfast order of an omelette. Rather than eat it here amidst foreign trekkers, I carry my plate to the more intimate kitchen where I know it will be warmer with the roaring fire in the stove. Besides, I am more comfortable here. Three Tibetans negotiate with Lhakpa over a pile of dried mutton carcasses. Sherap watches them, thoughtfully twisting strands of his moustache. He offers me a cup of milk tea and I sit down on a wooden stool and watch the bargaining process. The sides of mutton are so desiccated they would barely be recognisable as sheep carcasses if it weren't for the hooves. The negotiation is intense, the faces of the Tibetan traders pinched in concentration as Lhakpa squeezes the dried meat to determine its quality. To sell so many sides of sheep in one contract is important to these traders and the significance is reflected in their eyes as they look from Lhakpa to the mutton, and then back to Lhakpa. But Lhakpa is fair and a deal is finally struck.

The Tibetans leave, happy to have sold their remaining carcasses. Market day is over and it is time for them to head home, back to Tibet. Outside the sounds of the ringing yak bells mingle with the high-pitched yells of the caravan drivers as they pass by the lodge, returning to the mountain passes that will take them back to Tibet before winter effectively closes the border. One heavy snowfall and the passes will be sealed until spring. Through the kitchen window I see the drivers flail their arms and occasionally pick up a stone to throw at the animals loaded with heavy bags of rice and other goods.

Lhakpa, in Sherpa dress and apron, is the epitome of the professional hostess: unflappable, polite and smiling despite the pressure of dealing with the gastronomical demands of her Western guests. When she sees the egg omelette I have ordered, she insists I eat a proper Sherpa breakfast with them, as their guest. Again, I am served buffalo momo soup. It's amazing to think that since yesterday evening, a full sixty meals were produced from this medieval kitchen, with only one "burner" over a clay oven, and an additional kerosene stove.

When I had arrived at her lodge, I had told Lhakpa that I wished to hire a porter for up to twenty days to go to Everest Base Camp and Gokyo Lakes. On this morning she introduces me to Kumar, a Rai, about thirty years old, whom she has summoned from Namche to meet me. Unlike the earnest Chandra Rai, Kumar is older, restrained, and more experienced. He smiles politely as Lhakpa serves him a bowl of momo soup, perhaps to give him the sustenance he needs to start our trip. He can understand a bit of basic English, although he pretends otherwise. With my smattering of Nepali we'll do fine, although we won't be having philosophical talks along the trail. I tell him we will leave for Khunde at ten o'clock.

After packing my bag, I head down to the bakery to say goodbye to Ben, Caroline and Genevieve. I order a freshly ground coffee and a *pain au chocolat* and listen to them describe how they had slept on the floor in the prayer room of the lodge. I'm not sure if that is an auspicious occasion or not, given the circumstances. Caroline seems tired, sad, distracted. Genevieve has an expression on her face that speaks for females of any species after they have succumbed to the protracted lustful advances of the male: not so much contentment, as relief that it's over. But Ben has that enduring smile smeared across his face. And they still have not decided what they are about to do. Caroline is definitely flying out of Lukla if she can get on a flight, which is a given now that there are fewer trekkers heading out. Most have already gone by now. Ben is confirmed on a flight, so he's safe. Genevieve is still debating whether she will walk all the way down to Jiri to catch the bus out.

The dining room at the Panorama is empty of trekkers. They have all either moved on up towards Everest, or down to Lukla. Only a white-haired man sits there, unruffled by the lateness of his start.

"Dr. Sandy Scott," he introduces himself. "I'm heading up to Pheriche. Takes me two days from here. Not exactly what the guide books recommend, or the doctors at the Himalayan Rescue Association in Pheriche. But I don't seem to be one of those people who suffers from altitude."

Sandy Scott, I learn, has served as the doctor on several Everest expeditions and been as high as the South Col. He has also worked in the clinic at Pheriche and is heading up there now with the architectural plans to expand the basic health centre run by the Himalayan Rescue Association.

"In my career as a doctor, there are few occasions where I can say definitively that I saved someone's life," he tells me. "But each of those occasions has been here in the Himalayas. I've probably saved the lives of three or four trekkers with severe altitude sickness by putting them in a Gamow bag and helicptering them out. They wouldn't have made it through the night if I hadn't been there. One, a heavy man with a paunch, went straight up to Gorak Shep in a group and had a bad case of high altitude cerebral oedema. He was ataxic, couldn't even stand up. We had a porter carry him down to the hospital at Khunde where he argued over the fifty-dollar fee the porter charged him. Imagine. He had a moneybag full of cash wrapped around his belly and he argued about paying the fifty dollars that had probably saved his life." Sandy shakes his head, remembering. "Believe me, I've seen all kinds here."

We finish our teas and get up to leave.

"Things changed a lot since you first came here?" I ask as we walk out into the bright sunshine.

"That would be an understatement," Sandy replies. "Sherpas have become very modern and cosmopolitan. They've been introduced to an elite Western culture and adapted to it enthusiastically."

In the courtyard, I make the final adjustments to what I will carry and what Kumar will carry for me. While juggling items around I overhear a couple in the courtyard arguing with their potential porter.

"Five hundred rupees per day is too much," the husband clad in Mountain-Coop Equipment gear tells their prospective porter.

"Okay, four hundred and fifty rupees is no problem," the desperate porter replies.

"That's still too much," the wife says. "Three hundred rupees." She is wearing a matching Mountain-Coop Equipment Goretex jacket.

"Four hundred and twenty five is OK," the porter replies.

"No."

"Okay, three hundred rupees," the porter says amiably. "No problem."

"But you pay your own food and lodging," the husband now tells the distraught man. "And if we find another porter we like better, then we take him. We pay only day by day, as long as we like you, we pay. If we don't like you, then we don't pay you any more and you go."

I bite my tongue. It's all I can do. Then I go back inside the lodge and say goodbye to Sandy, Lhakpa, Sherap and Rema the Tamang girl.

Kumar hefts my pack, with his smaller bundle of personal possessions tied on top, and leads me around the perimeter of Namche, past the *gompa*, and up the steep sides to the ridge, past the Syangboche airstrip to Khunde. This village is not on the direct route to Everest Base Camp, which is one of the reasons it appeals to me. Although there is no *gompa* in Khunde, there is a hospital which I've heard a lot about, and I'm curious to see what it offers. It's a pleasant walk, and not having to carry my heavy pack makes the two-hour walk a boondoggle.

Distances walked each day at high altitude should be restricted to a daily vertical ascent of three hundred metres or less to reduce the risk of altitude sickness. It doesn't take long to climb three hundred metres. Khunde is four hundred metres higher than Namche and although I have spent three nights at Namche, I still suffer headaches during the nights. When I arrive at the Khunde hospital, I remove my daypack and sit with my back to the sunlight to dry the perspiration on the back of my T-shirt. The sky is cloudless, quite different to those black-grey clouds pressing in on Lukla. It's hard not to feel elated in this sharp mountain air with bright sunlight warming the day.

The Sherpa medical assistant who has worked at the Khunde hospital for several years shows me around the hospital. "Hospital" is a bit of a misnomer for the basic facilities available, but it does have an X-ray machine, and simple surgical operations are carried out here.

"Doctors in?" someone asks hopefully. I look up to see another trekker in the doorway, an attractive woman, very fit and athletic.

"Later," the medical assistant tells her. She steps back into the glaring sunlight as he deals with a patient who has just arrived.

"I'm Andrew."

"Jackie."

"Going up, or down?" I ask.

"Going up, with a group."

"Where are they?" I look around.

"In Namche," she says. "I came up to acclimatise and get away from them. I'm the group doctor." She sees the look of surprise on my face. "It's a bit of overkill for a mixed bag of wealthy clients. We've got a staff of about forty porters, guides, *sirdars*."

Another doctor. This one English, but living in Hong Kong.

"And you're sleeping in tents?"

"Yes, identical bright yellow tents," she says, wrinkling her nose as if remembering the awful sight of them. "You a doctor too?"

"No, just interested in seeing the hospital."

From the hospital, we have a view over the village. I recognise Laxmi below, winding her way towards us between stone walls and buildings.

"Thought I'd find you here," she says when she reaches Jackie and me. I introduce the two women. There seems to be a preponderance of medical people who come to the Himalayas, including a high proportion of doctors, nurses, physiotherapists, and occupational therapists. On the other hand, you don't meet a lot of accountants, actuaries or lawyers.

Jackie says goodbye and heads back down to Namche. We have the same itinerary up to Gorak Shep, just before Everest Base Camp.

"See you on the path," she says, before she disappears.

I turn to Laxmi. "I thought you were heading directly up to Gokyo?"

"Changed my mind this morning."

"Where's your pack?"

"I got myself a porter this morning," she says, looking back over the path she's just come up. "But now I can't find him. Haven't seen him since Namche. Where are you staying?" she asks.

"I was thinking of the lodge there," I say and I point at a nearby building. "So it's easier to meet the two Western doctors who work here, when they arrive."

"Can I stay there with you?"

"Go ahead."

"When I got to Khumjung, the village just over there, I phoned down to Namche to find out where my porter was," Laxmi explains her request. "The owner of the lodge told me my porter was on his way up. But the owner also told me that creep Mark, the self-proclaimed *Namche Doctor,* had asked where I had gone and apparently he's on his way up to Khumjung too. I don't feel very happy about it. It's like he's stalking me."

It's already early afternoon. We walk the thirty metres or so to the first lodge. A Sherpa is sitting outside the door.

"Room, cha?" I ask him.

"Cha," he replies, deadpan.

"Can we see?" I ask, in simple English.

"Sure." He gets up and shows me an immaculate room.

"Do you have dormitories?" Laxmi asks.

"Yes."

"How much is it for a bed in the dormitory?" she asks again.

I never think of asking the price. Even in the luxurious accommodation at the Panorama Lodge, my single room with a double bed cost one hundred rupees, less than a dollar and a half. The cost of the rooms, for all intents and purposes, is negligible.

"Sixty rupees."

"Okay," she says.

She just saved herself a dollar by sleeping in the dormitory rather than a room. But the owner surprises her.

"It's okay," he tells her. "There are no other people, so you can have a private room for the same price. Sixty rupees."

How incongruous to witness a surgeon from America saving a dollar while the relatively impoverished Sherpa is generous enough to give her a private room instead of the dormitory.

The owner leads us past dried yak dung stored against a stone wall in preparation for the winter. Next to the dung is a pile of dried sheep carcasses bought from Tibetan traders. Kumar puts my pack in a room, and I tell him I'm heading down to Khumjung with Laxmi to help her find her porter. The villages are so close together it's only a twenty-minute walk. Both villages are characterised by stone walls encompassing potato fields. The lodges for foreign trekkers are similar in structure to the traditional houses: square rectangular buildings made of stone with windows highlighted in paint, much like the windows of the Potala in Lhasa. While the older buildings have slate and timber roofs, the new lodges have corrugated tin, more numerous glass windows, and are made of stone and concrete rather than stone and mud mixed with straw. Like Namche, the Austrians have equipped the adjoining villages of Khunde and Khumjung with electricity and telephone, connected by underground cables. There isn't a single telephone pole or electrical pole in sight. Outside one traditional-looking house I see an electric bell ringer at a wooden gate in the perimeter wall. Not believing my eyes, I push the button and sure enough, within the house, I hear a loud electric bell ringing.

We wind our way between the shoulder-high stone stockades, past a long *mani* prayer wall, to Khumjung. I stare over the roof of the *gompa* at the foot of the Sherpa's sacred mountain of Khumbui Yul Lha, to the sky burial area that Suzanne had pointed out on the map. I touch my breast pocket to feel the envelope. It's there, safe. Over the past couple of days, with all the social events provided by friendly Sherpas and the local gossip of foreign trekkers, I've barely given the envelope much thought. But that's okay. I have plenty of time over the next couple of weeks to think about everything.

In Khumjung, Laxmi finds her porter. It had taken him just over an hour to climb up here from Namche, loaded with both of their packs. He is a young Rai, although he looks more like the lighter-skinned Mongolian-featured Sherpas. Only sixteen, he is somewhat intimidated working for a pretty young Western woman who looks Nepalese and has a Nepalese name.

Laxmi sorts through her pack in the courtyard of a lodge and I excuse myself to walk along another enormously long *mani* wall, just one of the many dry stone walls inlaid with engraved Buddhist prayer slates that line the paths. Scores of high school students stride towards me from their Hilary Foundation-supported school. They look and act like Western kids. Despite the rustic, Himalayan villages they live in, the students wear jeans, Western-style jackets and packs, running shoes. Many are cheeky as they walk by me, making rude remarks. At the end of the long *mani* wall, the longest I have seen, I hear a deep booming voice and recognise Bruce the Beard and his group again. They walk in a tight line, one behind the other, their retired schoolteacher guide leading them. Spotting me, they come over to chat.

"Staying here are you?" Bruce the Beard asks.

"No, up at Khunde," I reply, pointing at the village some hundreds of meters away. "Are you staying here?"

"Yeah."

I introduce Laxmi, who has caught up to me.

"She's a surgeon from New York," I tell him. Yesterday they saw me getting a back massage from Genevieve. "Have you got a doctor in your group?" I ask.

"Nah."

"Shouldn't travel in the Himalayas without a doctor you know," I say, goading him. "Altitude sickness and all that." I know I'm pressing all their buttons. It works.

"How much do you pay to stay in the lodges?" Bruce asks.

"Between sixty and one hundred rupees."

"And how much are you paying your porter?"

"Five hundred rupees per day," I reply.

I can see him mentally adding up the figures. I know he's seen the modest cost of the food on the menus in the lodges when they order. I don't know what Bruce has paid for his trip, but it certainly wasn't in the range of ten to twenty dollars a day, which is what I am spending. They're staying in the same lodges and eating the same food. They have porters to carry their bags, and an Australian guide, but I'd hazard a guess that they are paying closer to one hundred dollars a day for essentially the same services while I have the freedom to choose my friends, where I stay, and how far and how fast I go.

Laxmi and I walk back up to Khunde, her porter following us. He wears a Chicago Bulls baseball cap, a Nike windbreaker, Nike running shoes, and Levi jeans. Like Yes Yes Shelley's porter, he'll be Laxmi's only companion for the duration of the trek.

Back in the Shangrila Lodge in Khunde we sit down to talk to the owner, Chuldrin. I am embarrassed I had spoken to him in pigeon English. His English is excellent. He has been to America a number of times, once for three months, more recently, for five months. In fact, he has been back only a week. He's dressed neatly in pressed slacks, new running shoes, a fancy T-shirt and an immaculate windbreaker. He has a scarf wrapped dandily around his neck and his hair is neatly combed. He could easily pass himself off as an American as he sits there in the dining room with us, talking about his trips around the United States. His wife, on the other hand, is definitely a Sherpa/Tibetan with her heavy traditional dress and colourful apron. Although she is a good seven years younger, she looks ten years older than him. The tough life, cold winters and hard labour, have taken a toll. Her calloused hands are the hands of a woman old enough to be her mother, and her face is severely lined. While Chuldrin is spotlessly clean, as if he just came out of a shower, her hands are stained, her face smudgy with grime from the stove fires. She is only twenty-six, the same age as her American guest Laxmi, who looks as if she could be her daughter.

"Do you miss America?" I ask Chuldrin.

He places both hands over his face, then behind his head, and leans back. He doesn't reply for a moment. His response to my question is emotional, so much so it looks as if he is about to cry. His wife brings us our soup. She seems troubled and unhappy. It is hardly surprising. From what her husband tells us, he isn't thrilled to be back. He has seen the sophistication of another world, or other people, and returning home to his lodge in a tiny Himalayan village is too much of a jolt.

"American friends sponsored me and took me everywhere," Chuldrin says, to answer my question. "Sometimes I worked putting down tiles in their house. The house has many bedrooms, and each with a bathroom. Each tile for the bathrooms cost fifteen dollars. Each tile! I was paid for every hour that I work. Here, I sit doing nothing. In America, everyone is working hard, but here I cannot work like in America. In America, each hour is important. Here, one day or one week or one month, it doesn't matter. Now I find I'm very boring. I don't like Nepal. In America everyone works hard together. Here, government officials sit in offices reading the newspaper, drinking tea. They do not work. They do not pull together for the good of the country. Government officials here block your way unless you pay them a bribe. They do not provide a service. They prevent you from working hard."

As he talks, his foot bounces up and down with manic energy. In the kitchen we hear sounds of pots being taken down, the rattle of utensils as his wife cooks dinner. Occasionally, she comes into the dining room to feed the space heater with more wedges of yak dung. I imagine the look I see on her face is dejection.

"Did you bring anything back with you?" I ask Chuldrin, hoping to digress from his comparisons of America and Nepal, a conversation that so obviously upsets his wife with its harsh comparisons of Nepal to a country she will never visit.

Chuldrin nods enthusiastically. "Here you can get anything cheap, made in China. But some things I brought back from America. A caulking gun for my tiling job, I brought back to fix the leaks in the roof of my parents' house. And also kneepads for protection for working on my knees. These things I have never seen before."

"And those teddy bears?" I ask. I had noticed several immaculate teddy bears hanging from nails on the wall, near the ceiling. "Why do you keep them on the wall?"

"So that children don't take them outside and get them dirty."

The teddy bears look spotless, but they don't look as if they've had much fun hanging up there either.

"So, how is it being back?" Laxmi repeats my question. Again, Chuldrin puts his hands in front of his face, and then behind his head, and leans back. He is clearly distraught.

"Difficult, very difficult. I can't explain. I cannot tell you how lucky Americans are." He is fighting back the emotions. "I would like to change things here but... it is difficult now not working hard, not being paid by the hour. I want to go back."

"Everyone has difficulty going back to where they belong," I tell him, but he's not listening.

"I will return in May," he says, "during the monsoons, for three months. I will try to find work and save a couple of thousand dollars, if only my sponsors can give me free fooding and lodging."

Nepalese are always on the lookout for a 'sponsor', a wealthy visiting trekker who will subsidize an overseas trip, acting as a guarantor for a visit to Europe or the US. Or else a sponsor to pay for the education of their children in a private school in Kathmandu, or a benefactor who will commit to sending over cash every year.

Chuldrin's wife is back in the dining room eager to serve us fried finger chip potatoes. She knows very well what her husband is talking about although she can hardly speak English herself. She hovers around us, her sad face watching his every move. Studying the husband and wife, judging them by their appearance, the clothes they wear, their interaction, you would never guess that they were married. Chuldrin could be a visiting tourist, like us. Like Chombi and Sherap, he has worked all his life in the trekking industry, toiling his way up from porter to *sirdar*. Recently he worked for Great Escapes as a *sirdar*. I ask him about wages.

"I am paid monthly, but not much," he tells us. "But for each group I am given four thousand dollars to cover all the expenses of fooding and lodging for the clients. If I can save any money out of this, then it is mine. My father was a cook for climbing expeditions for twenty years. When I was in America I went to the anniversary of the first American expedition to climb Everest. My father was the cook on that expedition. I didn't know until I saw him in the photographs. He never told me. All the expeditions were the same for him."

It is easy to talk to Chuldrin. His English is good, he has travelled extensively, and he understands Westerners.

"How long have you had the lodge?" I ask.

"It belongs to a friend. I lease for one and a half years and my wife is running it while I am away leading trekking expeditions. I have a small apartment in Kathmandu that I rent for seven hundred rupees a month. It is only a room with two beds and nothing else but if my brother or I are there, then we can use it to sleep. We store our trekking equipment there too."

"For trips here in the Khumbu?"

"All over Nepal, even to Tibet I have been five times, including Mount Kailash. I feel very religious when I go to Tibet because Tibetan people are very religious, especially around Mount Kailash."

"Do you pay a lot to rent this lodge?" I ask, curious.

"Fifteen thousand dollars."

"A year?"

"Yes."

I consider how stressful it must be to have to make that much money in a season, just to cover the costs of leasing the building. Calculating it quickly in my head, it doesn't seem to me he'd ever make a profit unless he, or one of his American friends, was subsidising the effort.

"What else did you do before you had the lodge?"

"I was guide," Chuldrin says. "My wife looked after our small farm. We harvest potatoes in September and store the potatoes in the ground, then we remove them from the ground to make them dry and put them back again. We also have buckwheat."

"How did you meet your wife?" Laxmi asks.

"She's from Khumjung, but we went to the same school."

"The Hilary school?"

"Yes."

"Was it an arranged marriage or a love marriage?" I ask.

"A love marriage."

His wife enters, carrying yak dung, dried on an exterior wall for a month and then stored inside. She places several pats in the space heater and pours a small amount of kerosene on the dried turd to set the fire going. The sun has gone down and it quickly becomes cold. Laxmi's porter sits conspicuously close to her. Chuldrin puts a cassette in a small boom box and switches on the electricity, for which he pays the lodge rate of six hundred rupees per month. It's a cassette of tunes from the West.

"I have five older brothers and two older sisters," he says above the music, as if more to himself than to us. "In our culture, it is the youngest son who has responsibility for the parents."

A phone rings, startling me from gazing into the yak dung flames. I still can't get over the juxtaposition of modern technology with a medieval setting. Chuldrin goes nonchalantly over to the counter to answer the telephone as if he has been doing it all his life. It is the owner of the lodge in Namche on the line asking if Laxmi's porter arrived. Somehow, she not only knew that Laxmi had changed lodge, but also the village and lodge she is staying in. Laxmi takes the phone and confirms that her porter is indeed here. She listens intently, and then thanks the caller for the information.

"Mark is heading up the Gokyo Valley, looking for me," she says. She slumps beside me on the bench seat. "Sure you don't want to do the Gokyo Valley first? I really don't want to be alone if he catches up to me."

"No, sorry," I say.

"Then maybe I should come up to Everest Base Camp with you."

I don't reply to this suggestion. I really don't want to share this trip with anyone else. Chuldrin pre-empts any further discussion by handing us an enormous photo album given to him by his American friends, the ones who sponsored his visit to America. He met the husband and wife when he was the leader of a trekking group they were on.

The first photographs reveal a tall American man and his wife. They are holding up an enormous banner saying, *You Made It, Hip Hip Hooray!* Chuldrin is beaming under a cowboy hat. There are photos of him on Wall Street in New York, at other tourist spots in the Big Apple, in the surf at the beach, on a whale-watching boat trip. His host is a captain with Delta Airlines. There's even a photo of Chuldrin sitting in the co-pilot's seat and another in business class, being served by a stewardess. The captain's son is also a pilot, flying F-16 fighters. There are photos of Chuldrin at air shows, cocktail parties, at a Colorado ski resort, a rodeo, fancy cabins in the woods, on a Harley Davidson. The last photo shows him on a NOLS climbing course. That explains the certificate on the wall, just beyond the telephone, proof that he had completed the National Outdoors Leadership School. I wonder what his wife thinks, when she sees these exotic pictures.

Chuldrin also spent a year in Japan, and on another occasion three months there working in a factory. He has travelled more extensively than many Westerners and has mixed with an elite segment of North American society. Laxmi is thinking the same thing I am. She says, "You know most Americans haven't seen or experienced what you have? Most don't fly business class, or go to Wall Street, or watch whales, or take outdoor leadership training courses."

Chuldrin shrugs.

"You have children?" Laxmi asks him.

"This boy and a daughter." He points at a woven cradle in the corner of the room with a blanket draped over it. The baby has been so silent we didn't even know there was a baby there. A man who is obviously mentally retarded, comes into the room. He smiles at us, and plays with the baby boy in the cradle.

"His brother is the same way," Chuldrin tells Laxmi and me. "He is in the hospital but the doctors cannot find what is the sickness." The man points at the two children, then at himself before raising two fingers. He is telling us he has two children of his own. By contrast to Chuldrin, the man seems incredibly happy and uncomplicated. We watch as he plays tirelessly with Chuldrin's youngsters.

"I saw students today at the Hilary high school in Khumjung," I tell Chuldrin. "What do most of them expect to do when they finish studying?"

"That depends on the parents," Chuldrin replies.

"Alright then, what would you hope for your children?"

Chuldrin doesn't need to think long. He knows the answer well.

"That they become something better than me," he says. "I was only a porter when I left school. Now I have a lot of expectations for my children, but it depends on what I can support. Maybe a doctor, or a pilot, if I can save enough money for them. Before, I thought a pilot was like a god. But everyone in America is a pilot. It is easy to get a pilot's licence."

Chuldrin's wife serves us fried noodles. I think of how excited she must have been to have her husband back after five months without him. Instead, she is married to a stranger dressed in expensive running shoes, a sleek windbreaker, with a scarf wrapped around his neck; a man who barely looks at her.

The phone rings again and Laxmi panics.

"What if it's Mark?" she asks. "What if he's calling to say he's on the way over?"

But Chuldrin talks on the phone for several minutes before he hands the telephone to his wife. Unlike her husband, it's clear she is still not used to the apparatus. She holds the receiver timidly, staring at it, as if that will facilitate the communication process. But when she starts talking, her whole disposition changes. She smiles and laughs. She is suddenly proud and happy.

"Her brother," Chuldrin explains, "He has just returned to Khumjung from Oregon, where his sponsors live."

Later, our food eaten and before we say goodnight, I ask Laxmi about the mentally disabled man who so lovingly played with the children. He's the father of two children himself and I wonder whether he would necessarily have mentally deficient children. But Laxmi tells me no.

"It's probably because his mother used iodine when she was pregnant," she explains.

I have trouble sleeping. I can't forget how Chuldrin's wife beamed to hear her brother's distant voice. She is happy that her brother travels the world while she remains home, cleaning and cooking for her husband, when he's there, filling the stove with yak dung. But I guess her brother, unlike her husband, accepts her for who she is. But perhaps I'm being presumptuous.

Like Chuldrin's wife's brother, Kevin accepted me for who I am. I think he was even proud of the decisions I made, to opt out of a business career, to seek a life of adventure. After graduate school, with a degree in international economics, and an auspicious start as an economist in the economics department of two of Canada's largest banks, I took a sidestep to join the United Nations despite advice from my boss that it wouldn't do my career any good. From there I slipped even further down the path less travelled when starting up a safari business. While I was never motivated to make money, Kevin built up a publishing business, bought a house right on the South Shore on a private beach in Bermuda. I admired him for pursuing his goals. While I gallivanted around, he was building up his equity and had started a family. My only asset was my freedom and although it was a question of choice, I sometimes wondered if Kevin was jealous of the one thing I had that he didn't.

Despite my freedom, the solitude of this place reinforces the loneliness I feel at losing my brother.

Twice during my restless night, I step outside to urinate. Khunde is deathly quiet now. With a full moon hanging overhead I can easily see the valley below, and the swell of the mountains above.

8

Khunde-Tengboche Monastery

The Khunde hospital, funded in large part by the Himalayan Trust, is well known for providing exceptional service at these upper reaches of human habitation. In the morning Laxmi and I, both curious to see its facilities, walk up to the hospital. There were no other trekkers in Khunde overnight. It's amazing how easily one can step off the beaten path, even here in the Khumbu. It's before hospital hours when we arrive, so we go to the doctors' residence and knock on the door. I have already learned from the medical assistant that the doctors are a married couple, American, from somewhere in the Midwest. A tall woman opens the door. Her legs are unbelievably long and her blonde hair is in pigtails. Her jeans slide down her bony hips despite a wide cowboy belt buckle. She looks as if she forgot to strap on her sharpshooter. She reminds me of a stretched-out version of Annie Get Your Gun.

Are you one of the doctors?" I ask. She nods, frowning.

"We're not open until nine," she says curtly.

"We thought you might be too busy once you opened your hospital doors, so we came early," I tell her. "Laxmi here is a doctor."

"We don't talk to trekkers before nine, even if they are doctors," she replies.

Crestfallen, we walk back to the lodge. I had been looking forward to meeting the two Khunde doctors.

At nine Laxmi and I return to the hospital.

"We don't want to disrupt your work schedule," I say quickly to Annie Get Your Gun. "I'm sure you're busy."

Laxmi and I are waved inside where we meet Annie's doctor husband. He resembles a gangly schoolboy with pimples, a boy who might wish to grow up to become a doctor. Someone, probably Annie herself, put a bowl over his head and cut whatever hair stuck out.

It soon becomes clear that both these Khunde doctors, Annie and her husband, are fed up with visiting trekkers and doctors wanting to help. They do not suffer fools gladly.

"Doctors should just stay at home and practice their medicine there," Annie says. "All they do is come in for a day, or week, or month, and then leave again."

Her verdict seems a bit harsh.

"Not everyone can afford the time to volunteer for two years," I reply. "Maybe they'd like to do something to help in the short time they have."

"Well, they should all stay at home anyway," her husband snaps. "It makes our job that much more difficult. They come here, do their good deed for the day, and then take off and we're left holding the bag. They disrupt the long-term medical services we provide by interfering in the short term like that."

Laxmi has been quietly listening.

"Do you know Mark, the doctor down in Namche?" she finally asks.

"The *Namche Doctor* as he likes to call himself," Annie replies with sarcasm. "He's a real pain. There are so many lost souls, including doctors, wandering around this country, trying to figure out who they are. The US embassy staff call their Kathmandu post *Flake Mission* because there are so many Americans, guys predominantly, who flake out big time and have to be shipped home. Mark is typical. Exaggerating who he is and what his qualifications are. There are rumours that he screwed up big time in the States and that's why he's floating around out here. The local police are after him now because he climbed Island Peak without a permit."

"But he tells everyone he was the expedition doctor," Laxmi says, and she seems genuinely surprised.

"He asked to join them," the husband explains, "but his name wasn't on the list of climbers on the permit. So now he's in trouble with the police."

"Good," Laxmi replies.

"Oh?" Annie raises an eyebrow.

"He's been harassing me," Laxmi tells her. "He even came into my dorm late one night and asked if I wanted a back massage. Now he's stalking me up here."

"He's a nutcase," Annie says, nodding. We seem to have won her over a bit by sharing our dislike of Mark. "He comes onto the women big time. We've heard a number of complaints about him and much worse stories than yours. You can imagine," Annie says, "how he could easily abuse the trust he is given as a doctor."

To get off the subject of Mark the Flake, I make a passing reference to the incredible infrastructure of the tiny village of Khunde, including a hospital with two doctors, underground electricity and telephone wires. There can't be much more than a hundred local inhabitants here.

"Some of these people are wealthier than we will ever be," the husband tells us. He is not interested in discussing the social atmosphere of the village.

I'd heard so much about the Khunde Hospital but it's not the most productive of meetings. And it's obvious they want to get on with their day.

"Thank you for your time," I tell them. "We should be off. I need to reach Tengboche."

"Takes two hours," Annie Get Your Gun says. "Even my mother who came to visit only took five hours and she's in her seventies."

With that, she effectively dismisses us, although there are no patients in the hospital.

Laxmi and I leave Khunde and walk through Khumjung, hoping the errant Mark won't spot us. I look up at the Khumjung *gompa* and the Sherpa holy mountain of Khumbui Yul Lha towering overhead. A peak almost six thousand metres above sea level, no one has been allowed to climb this sacred mountain overlooking the villages of Khumjung, Khunde, Thame, Phortse, Pangboche, and Chukhung where most of the high altitude Sherpas come from. Above Khumjung is the sky burial ground that Suzanne in Kathmandu recommended as a spiritual spot to cremate the contents of my envelope.

Sky burials, where a human corpse is cut into pieces and placed on a mountaintop, exposing it to the elements and animals, especially birds of prey, is a practical means to dispose of human remains where fuel and timber are scarce and where the ground is too hard and rocky to dig a grave. But swept up with Laxmi's wish to avoid Mark, I put the thought of burning the envelope to the back of my mind and keep walking. This place doesn't quite have the appeal I had expected to say my final farewells to Kevin. Besides, I've only just started this pilgrimage and I hope to find somewhere more appealing higher up the valley.

We descend from Khumjung to Sanasa. The path splits and we stop.

"Are you sure you don't want to go to Gokyo first?" Laxmi suggests again.

"I'm sure." I really want to do this trip on my own.

"I wish I had an older porter like yours," she says then. "Mine seems a bit jumpy." She studies her Rai porter sceptically and then turns to head up the path, climbing a steep stone staircase. Her tight-fitting climbing pants accentuate her slim figure. Following close behind is the eager young porter. I can't help but feel relieved that I don't have the same problems with a hormone-driven Kumar. I watch them ascend the path carved out of the vertical rock face and hope that Mark the Flake won't track her down.

Kumar and I cross the Dudh Kosi River. At an empty stretch of trail I stop and look back to the thin turquoise ribbon of river flashing brightly through the valley. The perpendicular sides of the valley are so steep and narrow that a natural stone arch has formed where a massive boulder has tumbled and jammed into the clefts of rock. Staring down the narrow defile that is the impregnable portal to the upper Dudh Kosi valley, it's obvious why we had to detour along the Bhote Kosi, to Namche, in order to ascend to Everest Base Camp.

Further up the trail, we come upon a man repairing the path. He stops work to accost a trekking group, demanding that they pay cash into a large wooden box for the maintenance of the trail. They quickly do what he asks. I do too, to avoid the verbal abuse he hurls at two individual trekkers who walk past, nonchalantly. But the repair of the path is a ruse I had been warned about, thanks to a writer/photographer friend of mine in Kathmandu. Chris Beall had forewarned me that the earth shuffled from one side of the path to the other was the most shovelled clump of earth anywhere in Nepal, if not the world. "It's a scam," said Chris. "The guy's been shovelling the same pile of dirt for years." The ploy has worked well, earning the swindler a small fortune.

After crossing the river at Phunki Tenga, I begin the long climb up to Tengboche monastery. It's hot and dusty in the intense sunlight, so I stop to remove my daypack and take off my fleece jacket. I still have disconcerting pains in my back. Half-a-dozen well-built men with enormous packs walk past us.

"Andrew?" a voice asks. I woman carrying a sizeable backpack, stares intently at me.

It takes a few seconds before I recognise the face.

"Christina," she says, jogging my memory.

"New Zealand?" I ask, astonished. She quickly nods. I can't believe it.

"Christina, what are you doing here?"

"I was going to do the Annapurna Circuit but met these British soldiers in the Irish Bar in Kathmandu," Christina explains. "They persuaded me to join them to Everest Base Camp instead. We've walked up from Jiri. I can't believe bumping into you here."

Another solidly built man walks by slowly, studying me as he passes.

"Neither can I," I say. We met in Te Anau, New Zealand, three years ago. She was a nurse from London, and I had lent her some of my equipment while she walked the Milford Track and I the Kepler. She had a car and gave me a lift from Christchurch, then on to Kaikoura. We spent some days together and like travellers do, we talked a lot, and shared a lot.

We continue on together now, up the path, accompanied by one of the British soldiers who sticks so close to Christina that he is privy to our conversation.

"Did you get into medicine?" I ask. She had intended to go back to school to study to become a doctor, like her father and brothers.

"I didn't in the end," she says. "After New Zealand I went to Australia and met a Dutch guy, so I stayed there for a time. But when we went home to Europe, it wasn't the same."

Perspiration drips off our faces as we climb up the hill to Tengboche. Christina asks about each member of my family. She finally gets to Kevin. "How is your brother? He has two children, doesn't he?"

"Katie and Cooper," I tell her, amazed that she can remember such details. But I offer nothing else. The walking uphill is difficult, an exertion, and I'm hoping the subject will end and that we will concentrate on the climb. But Christina wants to know about Kevin. "And your brother?" she asks again, "Kevin, right?"

"He died earlier this year," I say, and somehow the work needed to climb, the exertion, helps push the words out of me.

Christina stops in her track and takes hold of my arm.

"Oh Andrew, I am so sorry," she says. We step aside for a passing yak caravan. "Were you two very close?" she asks.

"In some ways," I say, but I'm reluctant to talk about Kevin in the midst of British soldiers and yaks and scam artists. "But we are, were, very different too."

"How old are his children?"

"Katie's four and Cooper is twelve."

"They must be devastated."

Christina doesn't say anything for a while as we struggle up the incline. When we stop to catch our breath, she asks, "You've been able to handle it, Andrew?"

"The reality takes time to sink in," I answer. We keep climbing. It's all I want to do now. I don't want to tell her what I know, what anyone who has lost someone they love knows, that one goes through a range of emotions. Anger. Sorrow. Regret. Frustration. I don't want to tell her that I wake up at night with this black pit in my stomach. For weeks after his death, I could barely function.

I stare down at my boots scuffling the dry dust.

"Eventually," I say, "There is a moment when you wake up and the awfulness isn't staring you in the face."

Christina looks out over the valley and says nothing. She understands that this is not a time for me to talk of Kevin. Some details one can never share. Such as the guilt I still feel.

I don't tell Christina about my other motives for coming here, about the envelope in my breast pocket.

A porter skips down the path, his empty carrying basket balanced on the back of his head.

"Where are you staying in Tengboche?" she asks.

"I don't know," I reply. "You're camping with the soldiers?"

"Not necessarily," she says, despite the handsome soldier chaperoning her, following her with the devotion of a puppy.

We turn a bend in the path and pass through a stone *kani*, an entrance arch with a row of prayer wheels on either side of the interior walls. Just as we reach Tengboche we see the incongruous sight of a helicopter nose protruding over the crest of the hill. The gleaming helicopter is in stark contrast to the crumbling *kani* walls and the faded, painted Buddhist images. Another yak caravan lumbers by loaded with a group's trekking gear.

Tengboche *gompa* is a huge building with several new edifices under construction. It looks rather grand, almost like a miniature of the Potala in Lhasa. Construction material, steel crossbeams, and long planks of timber are strewn in front of the *gompa*. Dilapidated lodges owned but leased out by the *gompa* border the open grassy pasture area. Two of these ramshackle lodges shelter the helicopter pad from winds scooting down the valley. It's a strange place, contrasting the ultra modern with the very traditional.

Men armed with film cameras climb into the helicopter as the turbines fire up and the blades begin to rotate. Several trekkers and Nepalese watch. The helicopter jets whine louder and the machine reluctantly hovers over the dusty ground. It does not take off so much as shudder forward to drop into the valley where it attains the forward momentum necessary to gain enough additional lift to become properly airborne.

Christina has disappeared, presumably with the British soldiers who establish their campsite on the other side of the grassy field. I walk through a strand of mature pine trees to a shabbily constructed lodge. But what it lacks in structure, it more than makes up for in outlook. I can see down the valley to the Everest View Hotel, the village of Khumjung, and the army headquarters on the hill above Namche. Behind I can see Ama Dablam and other massive Himalayan mountains, although it is not clear which one is Everest.

The proprietor shows me into a jerrybuilt bedroom. The room has a glass pane window providing a spectacular view down the valley. But the building is so close to the edge of the ridge edge that

I have just enough space to step outside the door. Another step forward and I'd be halfway to Namche. Kumar drops my pack on the wooden floorboards and I follow him into the medieval kitchen to order a soup and fried potato chips. A trekker reads beside the space heater in the dining room which doubles as a dormitory. I greet him but he doesn't reply. Plastic climbing boots, crampons, and not just one ice pick but two, signifying a serious climber, lie in a bundle at the foot of the bunk bed. Clearly he is not just a backpacking trekker like me, which might explain his aloofness.

To distract myself from the uncomfortable silence, I study a pamphlet describing the renovations taking place at Tengboche. Written by a German, it's very professional, a carefully worded document that provides a history of Tengboche, and a plan for the future, including drawings of the construction being undertaken. I learn that the Tengboche Monastery is not that old, first constructed in 1916. In 1934, an earthquake destroyed it. On January 19, 1989, the rebuilt monastery burned to the ground. Now it's in the process of a major reconstruction. The main building consists of a prayer hall, a *Do-khang*, dominated by a huge statue of Sakyamuni Buddha. Fifty monks live here and apparently some twenty-two thousand Western tourists visit Tengboche each year. A web site is listed with an e-mail address to facilitate the sending of donations.

I finish my meal and take my plates into the dark kitchen where Kumar sits, happily eating *dal bhaat* and playing with the owner's children. He does this at all the lodges, always eager to help and always ready to play with the little ones. He is proving to be an ideal porter, not encroaching on my space. Nepalese music spills out from a radio. I ask for a Snickers bar locked tantalisingly inside a glass-fronted cabinet. The cost of the chocolate is the same as the price of my room, and a third of Kumar's daily salary. I shove it guiltily in my pocket as I head outside to look around.

Strings of prayer flags flutter from memorial *chortens* erected to the memory of dead climbers. A black Tibetan raven caws as it glides effortlessly on the current of air sweeping over the ridge. Balancing its wingtips, the huge bird studies me with its beady black eyes. I unwrap the Snickers bar and eat it in tiny bites to make it last. The raven, hoping that I might drop a morsel, glides so close I could reach out my hand so he could snatch the chocolate bar from me with his enormous beak.

The view down the Dudh Kosi to the entrance of the Sagarmatha National Park is, as Jamie described, truly staggering. But although I have walked for some hours today, I am still at the same elevation as Khunde, just over 3,800 metres above sea level. Behind me the Imja Khola flows down from the Khumbu glacier. Across the valley, the path cuts spectacularly into the mountainside from Sanasa to Phortse Tenga and up towards Gokyo.

It is hardly surprising this ridge was chosen in 1916 as a site for an important *gompa*; it has a commanding view and would have made a strategic location for a fort, if anyone could have been bothered defending such a barren place. A *gompa* wasn't built here centuries ago for the obvious reason that no one lived here. Khunde and Khumjung and Phortse across the Imja Khola River were the uppermost villages. But with thousands of trekkers making the pilgrimage to Everest Base Camp, the higher yak summer pastures have been transformed into permanent villages, inhabited throughout the year.

At the end of a row of prayer flags, there is a memorial plaque dedicated to someone whose book I have read.

Russian Lhotse Expedition.
Vladimir Bashkirov.
28/01/52 – 27/5/97.
To a great climber and a dear friend.

There is no indication of who erected the plaque on this cairn. Yet, what sadness and pain must lie behind those simple words. Bashkirov was part of the Russian team that attempted to climb Lhotse, in the spring of 1997. Bad weather forced them back and it was on the descent that Vladimir Bashkirov, the strongest high altitude climber in Russia, died. He died just above the Russian Expedition Camp IV, one of ten climbers who summitted Lhotse without oxygen. He was descending with Anatoli Boukreev, who radioed that he needed supplemental oxygen for Bashkirov. Two teammates ascended from the Russian high camp with bottled oxygen, but it was too late. Bashkirov died soon after they arrived with the oxygen. He was forty-four years old. It pains me to imagine the suffering his death must have caused others, especially since it seems so futile: to die climbing a mountain just because it's there.

Thin streaks of cloud high above indicate the weather may change. A breeze blows and the prayer flags flutter, as if spirits were about. Suddenly, thumping rotors reverberate off the mountainsides. I spot a helicopter flashing brightly in the sunlight against the shadowy backdrop of mountains. Eventually it settles in a cloud of dust in front of the monastery. I head in that direction, to see what the commotion is all about.

A Japanese woman sits listlessly outside a lodge, an oxygen mask over her face. As I watch, two well-dressed Sherpa guides, sporting mirrored sunglasses, help her up and onto the chopper. Another carries the portable oxygen bottle. The massive blades of the helicopter keep rotating, and seconds after she has boarded, it takes off, rushing her down to lower levels in Kathmandu. There, hopefully, her high altitude problems will disappear.

As soon as the helicopter disappears, another helicopter emerges, flying up the valley to Pheriche, where two doctors are stationed at the Himalayan Rescue Association clinic. They, too, have radio contact with Kathmandu to call in a chopper when it's needed to evacuate patients. All the time, against the noise of the helicopters flying up and down the valley, are the steady taps of the stonemason hammers, and the sounds of great logs being sawed into planks as work continues on the new additions to the Tengboche monastery.

With time to spare, I begin climbing the steep crest overlooking Tengboche where snow and ice lies on the northern face of the mountain. I ascend the slippery spur to a relatively flat shelf where it is blissfully quiet.

This is what I came for.

But the silence is soon broken as the helicopter returns from up the valley, bringing down another sick trekker who has climbed too high, too fast. Now the sun disappears behind the mountains to the southwest. Despite the chill, I remain sitting on my hidden loft above the rest of the world. As evening approaches, the activity around the lodges and *gompa* dissipates. Sunlight illuminates the tops of the Himalayas to the north and east, catches the edges of Thamserku to the south, and lights up the impressive monolith of Ama Dablam. Below, floodlights illuminate Tengboche monastery. It's an odd sight, this floodlit *gompa* nestled amidst the Himalayas, ten days walk up from the nearest road and yet connected to the outside world by electricity, telephone, and the Internet. Prayer flags mounted on tall wooden poles flutter in the breeze, casting out their supplications with every tremble. Perhaps they're as effective as the Internet as a means of communication, at least when it comes to otherworldly things. Warm lights inside the lodges glow through windows. Hidden from view, I feel almost omniscient, and omnipresent, staring down at this surreal scene. Perhaps this is what it is like to be dead. Maybe we float in the murky cold, with a commanding overview of the earth below.

Weeks after Kevin died, it was as if he was still with me. I could feel his presence everywhere I went. I even began wearing his shirts. The envelope with his hair is in the breast pocket of a heavy plaid shirt of his that I am wearing now. It feels good to be wrapped in a something that belonged to my brother, enveloping myself with his presence, in something that once wrapped his body. Wearing his shirt I imagine it's as if I have donned a protective shield from the outside world.

Despite shivering with the cold, I linger on the spur of rock until the moon illuminates the snow-capped mountains on the valley opposite Namche. Behind, Ama Dablam points its enormous shadowy finger at the stars overhead. The moonlight is so strong, the sky so clear, that I can see the shadows cast by the moon over the mountains.

This is what I long for, to be free for a time of the lodges, the trekkers, the retinue of Sherpas and Rais. Now, I feel a presence and it's one I've felt in these mountains before. It's a benign presence. It's what I've been hoping for, expecting.

When the moon rises higher I am out of the shadows and can see my way back down the slippery ridge. I descend the icy path back to Tengboche. The presence follows me as I walk past the illuminated *gompa*, through the mature strand of pine trees. The moonlight is so intense I can see the colours of the trees. Everything is still. A couple of electrical lights twinkle in Khumjung and Khunde on the other side of the steep Dudh Kosi valley.

Too late to ask for something to eat, I crawl into my sleeping bag in my flimsy room at the foot of the Himalayas, far, far away from everyone I love. Cocooned in Kevin's shirt, and with his hair inches from my heart, through the window I can see the stars and the luminescent light of the moon shining on the snowy mountains.

The mountains seem close enough to touch.

9

Tengboche-Deboche
The Lost Porter

I wake invigorated. Through the frosted window I see the brightly illuminated tops of Kongde and Teng Kanpoche on the other side of Namche, overhanging the valley to Thame. The sunrise slowly reaches down their snow-covered slopes, changing colours from intense orange to bright yellow and, finally, a brilliant white.

As I walk into the dining room of the lodge, my footsteps wake the Non-Talkative Climber in the adjoining dormitory. I greet him *Bonjour,* but he ignores me as he packs his sleeping bag into his medium sized pack, pulls on his plastic climbing boots and, wearing shorts over his long blue thermal underwear, sets off in silence. He's on his own, so presumably he isn't about to summit a peak. But what will he do with two ice picks all on his own? Climb a frozen waterfall? I watch through the window as he looks up at the mountains, as if to assess the conditions. Maybe he's like Jamie, just wandering around the Himalayas, not necessarily climbing peaks, but crossing passes, finding solitude in more authentic spots than my little spur overlooking Tengboche. Two weeks earlier and he and I would have been fighting to find a bed in Tengboche. Now that it's December, the numbers of trekkers have diminished to the extent that he can be annoyed at having to share the lodge with anyone at all.

After breakfast I stroll over to the monastery. The prayer hall is closed until four in the afternoon and because the German Michael isn't around, there is no guided tour. It seems he is the only one who can give a tour nowadays. But the souvenir shop is open, selling Tengboche T-shirts, prayer flags, postcards. I pick up a string of prayer beads.

"You want?" the lama in saffron-and-ochre robes asks.

"They're plastic," I reply, studying the beads closely. I had thought of buying some, had they been wooden.

"You want wood prayer bead?" he asks, as if he could read my mind. Hell, maybe he can. He's a lama in a souvenir shop within a *gompa* after all. He reaches under his robes and pulls out very worn, stained wooden prayer beads. "You want?"

"Sure," I say, although I'm not. I wonder if they are his personal prayer beads.

"Five hundred rupees is okay," he suggests.

He takes my money and gives me the beads, then throws in a postcard of the resident *rinpoche* for free. I'm not sure if I should feel guilty for taking his prayer beads although I can be reasonably sure they aren't actually his.

I pocket them anyway and return to the lodge. Kumar has disappeared.

"Where is my porter?" I ask the lodge owner.

"Pangboche," he replies, without looking. He is busy fixing a radio.

"Kumar is in Pangboche?" Totally dependent on him to carry my pack, I can't leave. And yet, I don't want to hang around and spend a second night here either. I ask to pay my bill. The husband uses a calculator to add it up. Eight hundred and eighty rupees. I don't usually bother checking, but with plenty of time on my hands, this time I do. It adds up to only six hundred and eighty. He recalculates and arrives at the same sum I did. Six hundred and eighty, a difference of two hundred rupees. The disparity is only three dollars, insignificant, I know, but deliberately being cheated to one's face isn't pleasant.

Jamie had advised me to bypass Tengboche to a small community called Deboche. "There's a lodge there, the Ama Dablam, run by a woman called Mingma. I know you will be interested in talking to her, Andrew." Curious to know why Jamie would recommend her, I tell the lodge owner where I am going and ask him to let Kumar know where to meet me.

Without my backpack, I walk past the gamut of *gompa*-owned lodges rented to local Sherpas in order to generate income for the *gompa.* I head down the path through rhododendron forest festooned with Spanish moss. Snow lies on the ground where it's protected from the direct rays of the sunlight. It's a short walk to the three-story Ama Dablam lodge, situated on its own in a flat pasture surrounded by trees. Being late morning, trekkers who were there overnight have already gone, and it is too early for this evening's crew to have arrived.

In the empty kitchen of the lodge a well-dressed man sweeping the floors greets me. I ask for Mingma.

"I am Mingma," he answers.

"But I thought Mingma was a woman," I say.

"That Mingma is no longer here," he tells me. "She is in the lodge at Tengboche." He's yet another Sherpa, whose English is almost perfect. "You want a cup of coffee or tea?"

"Tea."

I follow him to a large clay fireplace with four burners. Even by the relatively high standards here in the Khumbu, this is a deluxe kitchen. Flames flicker out of the two openings from which logs protrude. A young boy comes in, twelve, maybe thirteen years old, his arms laden with wood, which he feeds into the stove. I had thought firewood was not allowed in the National Park.

"You've got a nice lodge here." I sit down at a wooden table with Mingma while his cook pours me a hot milk tea from a thermos. "Is it yours?"

"I rent it from a friend who works for a trekking company in Kathmandu," Mingma answers. "He doesn't have the time to run the lodge. You want to see it?"

He takes me into the spotless dining room with a space heater at one end, and at the other glass cabinets containing an assortment of chocolate, beer, Pringle potato chips, whiskey, and rum. The floor above has several rooms and a squat-type porcelain toilet. A sign outside the door says to use it only at night.

"We have to carry the water up here," Mingma explains, when he sees my puzzled look. "So it is easier if people use the toilets outside. But at night it's okay to use this one."

I look inside one of the single bedrooms and spontaneously decide to spend the night here although I have walked no distance at all. Mingma immediately pulls out a cordless telephone and rings the Trekkers Lodge in Tengboche. He tells them he is sending a porter to get my pack, and to let Kumar know where I am, whenever he returns from wherever he's been.

"How long have you had the telephone?" I ask as we return down to the kitchen. It still seems implausible, especially with the underground electricity and communication cables.

"Here in this lodge for two months, but in Tengboche for two years," Mingma tells me with evident pride. "I would like to own my own lodge," he says then, as we sit down at the table. The boy is working feverishly over the burners of the stove. "But that would cost so much money. It is no longer allowed to cut down trees inside the park so all the wood for construction has to come from Phakding. It is expensive to bring wood here from Phakding."

He pours me a cup of tea, steaming hot.

"And all the firewood you are using comes from outside the park?" I ask.

"We can use dead wood, but we cannot chop down trees," Mingma replies. "Some Rais come here and chop down trees in the forest and then come back and say the trees are dead. To solve this problem, revenue from tourism in the National Park could subsidise the cost of kerosene, then it would be easier and cheaper to use kerosene instead of wood." He shakes his head. "But we Sherpas who live here have never seen any money from the entrance fees to this park. The six hundred and fifty rupees tourists pay to enter this park go to the government treasury." He is clearly upset at this. "There is too much corruption. But the Communist Party in Namche has done a lot for us. They have obtained hundreds of thousands of rupees when we got nothing from the Congress Party." This thought makes him angry and his eyes narrow. "There are many rich in Nepal, but many Nepalese people don't know where the next meal is coming from each night when they go to sleep."

"And you, Mingma, what would your dream be?" I ask, hoping this will divert from his tirade against His Majesty's Government of Nepal. Communists or not, many Nepalese are so frustrated over the inefficiency and corruption of the Nepalese government that they have given the Maoists a significant power base. Even the Nepalese royal family no longer commands popular support, especially since the present King of Nepal took over from his brother who was tragically murdered by his drugged son.

"My dream would be to build a very good lodge like this, but at Lobuche," Mingma tells me. "I offered the owner of this lodge one hundred and fifty thousand dollars but he would not accept it." He looks about him. "For him, this is a good investment. The longer he keeps it, the more valuable it becomes. You cannot buy land now in the National Park, but you can lease it from the government, if you pay bribes. Maybe ten thousand dollars bribe. But it will be a good deal." Mingma shrugs his shoulders. "*Khe garne?*" he asks. What to do?

I repeat the rumours I'd heard about the German called Michael who runs the Tengboche Monastery.

"Is it true that he gives tours and keeps the money?"

"The Sherpa guides are jealous of Mike because they themselves can no longer show Tengboche monastery to their trekking groups," Mingma says. "Mike can explain Buddhism very well in English and German, much better than the trekking guides. Maybe he takes some of the money from the tours, but that also is good because he brings a lot of tourists. If he keeps some money, he can afford to continue to stay here. He also raises a lot of money from donors."

Two Sherpa women come in to have tea with us. The boy who has been hard at work now prepares lunch for them. Mingma sees me watching.

"The young cook is Santos Rai. He is an orphan who never saw his mother or father," Mingma tells me. "He came looking for a job. First he just fetched the water, sometimes carrying seventy litres from the tap to here, twenty times a day." I'm stunned. The child is barely over five foot. "Then he swept, cleaned and then assisted in the kitchen, and now he is paid two thousand rupees a month as assistant cook."

Thirty dollars. As far as I can see, he's actually the cook, dipping his hands into tins full of spices as he sprinkles a potpourri of herbs and spices into bubbling pots. He looks determined, with a ready smile and sparkling eyes.

My pack arrives, carried by a Caucasian-looking porter with dark skin. He is a Chetri. The Brahmins who are the priestly caste, and the Chetris who are the warrior caste, are at the top of the Hindu caste system. This poor Chetri has come up the desolate valley, far from his warmer village below, to look for casual work as a porter. I give him fifty rupees for carrying my pack, and disregard the niggardly thought of deducting it from Kumar's salary. The Chetri hovers around the lodge, carrying water and doing odd jobs, hoping for a lucrative job of carrying packs for trekkers, which is probably what Kumar is doing right now.

Mingma has bragged to me of his hot shower facilities and now I am curious to see them. Little Santos shows me a wooden shack out the back with a black plastic pipe that leads from the second floor of the lodge. He demonstrates how to operate the faucet before he scarpers off. I undress and wait in the wooden cubicle. Standing naked in the shadowy confines of a damp and bitterly cold shower stall on frozen floorboards does nothing for one's disposition. I play with the tap, thinking I may have got Mingma's instructions wrong. To keep my feet warm I throw my dirty clothes on the icy floor as insulation before I finally hear a gurgling. Hot water drips tantalizingly out of the faucet onto my head. It feels wonderful. I wet my body and soap up, constantly kneading the clothes under my feet to get maximum use of the hot water. I am well lathered when the dripping water stops. Shivering, and wondering what the hell has happened, I can't open my eyes with the soap dripping into them. I feel around for the tap and give it a shake. Nothing. Then I hear Santos yelling out a warning, *Tato pani*! He has just carried a second bucket of steaming water up from the kitchen, to the container on the second floor, and once again the hot water drips from the tap.

In the early afternoon I return up to Tengboche for the daily four o'clock prayer session in the gompa prayer hall. It's an easy half-hour walk from the lodge. On the way up to the gompa I pass a caravan of heavily loaded yak heading in the same direction. Their tongues stick out and their bellies pant with the effort. One grinds its teeth audibly as I walk by.

At one of the lodges in Tengboche I recognise the Australian group sitting morosely outside, their troupe of laughing guides and porters serving them lunch. Bruce the Beard pulls out a chair for me to sit.

"Been here long?" he asks.

"Since yesterday," I reply. "And you?"

"Ah yeah, just arrived, mate. Where are you staying?"

"In Deboche," I reply. "There's a really good lodge there. You could eat off the floors it's so clean. Porcelain toilet on the second floor. Hot shower facilities." I show him my hair, still wet under a baseball cap.

"Strewth!" Bruce the Beard shouts. "Now why can't *we* stay in the good lodges? We're paying enough as it is." He's on a whining roll. "This one's a dump."

"It's been a bad day for him," his wife warns.

"Porter must have broken my aftershave bottle on the way up here," Bruce explains. "Soaked my clothes. Bloody stink. I've a stomach upset and the pink Chinese toilet paper they sell? I reckon it's left thousands of splinters in me arse."

His wife takes over.

"And if you buy the rolls of white toilet paper," she adds, "they're so thin you might as well not be using them." She says this primly, screwing up her nose and wiping her hands on a hankie.

"Help yourself," Bruce says, and extends a tube of Pringles. "Won't touch the food here. One of us has had food poisoning already after eating something when we arrived. Garbage everywhere. Good thing this is our last night. Heading back out tomorrow."

"This is as far as you are going?" I ask. I think of the trip as just getting interesting at this stage.

"Yeah. For some of us it's not enough, and for others it's already been too much. One member of our group is still trying to catch us up. The younger ones wait hours every day for the rest of the group to arrive and then we have stragglers a day or two behind us." The husband and wife look at each other. It's her turn.

"We booked this almost a year ago," she complains. "We read about the trip from the written material our guide sent us, but there was nothing that could prepare us for this. Sure makes you appreciate home."

I look down the path and notice a raven as it lands on the back of a scraggly calf to peck away at something in the animal's hide. The calf seems to enjoy it. A retarded man walks around the open grounds as he picks up garbage and places it in a wicker basket slung over his back. Their Australian group's guide, a middle-aged Aussie woman, stands at the edge of the disgruntled team. She is staring through a pair of binoculars in the direction of Ama Dablam. I excuse myself from the disgruntled couple and go over to see what the guide is scrutinizing.

"Four climbers have almost reached the summit," she tells me, without looking away from the mountain.

Ama Dablam is easily the most impressive of the Himalayan peaks in sight and yet it is "only" six thousand eight hundred and fifty-six metres high. From this angle it seems to loom vertically overhead, its perpendicular flanks and knife-ridges hanging above fluted columns of snow. The guide hands me the binoculars. Sure enough, I see four specks, as if bits of black pepper have been blown against a background of white snow, and are now stuck against the upright ice face. Below the four specks is a huge crack across the entire width of the mountain peak, as if the summit was about to topple off. It's an impressive sight, awesome enough to witness from down here where I stand. It must be truly scary up there.

"You're heading back tomorrow?" I hand her back the glasses. She takes the binoculars and peers through them again, at the climbers.

"Yeah," she says. "First group I've led. I'm going to do it differently next time, cut out the middlemen. Already talked to our Nepalese guides about that. We'll deal with them directly. I mean, we've all seen what it costs to stay in the lodges, eat the food, and have porters and guides. We've been paying a substantial premium above those costs to the company that organised the trip in Australia, and their Nepalese tour operators here. Someone's making a lot of money off these clients and it sure isn't me. I reckon the real cost per client is something like ten, fifteen US dollars at the most, but they paid a lot more than that."

All the time, she is watching the specks on the mountain.

I spend the afternoon outside the lodge, sometimes watching the climbers on Ama Dablam, sometimes watching the trekkers around me. The climbers on the mountain are racing against time as clouds thicken until dark plumes hide the higher peaks. It is only a matter of time before the same clouds form over Ama Dablam. Already white wisps billowing off its stiletto top conceal the mountaineers as they reach the pinnacle of this mass of near vertical rock and ice.

A tightly packed group of Japanese arrives. They all sit down on a blue plastic tarpaulin spread out for them by their Sherpa guides. The clients diligently remove their hiking boots before they step politely in stockinged feet onto the tarpaulin and help themselves to cups of tea arranged neatly by their staff. But the whole delicate proceeding is mangled when several passing yak break away from their drivers and rumble through the middle of the genteel setting, like proverbial bulls in a china shop, scattering crockery and trekkers with equal alacrity. It is hard to know who panics more: the Japanese, the yaks, or the yak herders. Frightened shitless by all the confusion, the last yak stops in the middle of the tarpaulin to drop several ponderous turds. A refined Japanese tea party has been transformed into a chaotic mess, with tea and food and yak dung mashed into the plastic sheet by the enormous hooves. The Japanese clients scurry about in stocking feet as the yak are rounded up and herded away.

In the meantime, the climbers are momentarily visible on the top of Ama Dablam. The mountaineers are at the summit for only moments before they begin the steep drop to the huge crevasse that bisects the white Popsicle-top of this impressive peak. We watch them from below for another hour. There are no incoming news bulletins or radio reports, but we can easily surmise what is going on. They are in a race against the congealing clouds. The loftier peaks are already buried in dense black clouds that must be heavy with snow. A tiny orange tent is barely visible on a small, snow-covered shoulder. It looks as though the climbers will reach their tent just before the storm hits.

At four o'clock, two young lamas blow conch shells from an upper window to announce the prayer session to the fifty or so trekkers waiting outside the Tengboche *gompa*. The interior *gompa* doors are opened and we respectfully remove our shoes and boots before being admitted to the prayer hall. The enormous room is rich with shades of ochre and saffron, the walls covered in shiny *mandalas*, religious works of art brilliant in primary colours. Westerners huddle beside each other, sitting uncomfortably on the cold floor, backs propped against the wall. A procession of lamas walks in to sit at their designated places on raised wooden bench seats. They wear heavy woollen ochre robes to ward off the penetrating chill. A young lama pours each of them a glass of tea, the steam rising from the cups into the frigid shadows. The ages of the lamas' range from the head lama, who is probably in his fifties, to young boys who look as if they are barely ten. It's a relaxed atmosphere punctuated by a couple of young lamas who laugh and giggle at some esoteric joke. Cymbals and drums clash and bang. A boy thumps a large drum sporadically, and apparently at random. Equally discordant sounds are blown from a variety of oddly shaped horn instruments to create a cacophony of sound. I stay as long as I can, but my back cannot take the strain of sitting hunched in a ball with no support. Reluctantly, I climb over the other trekkers to the exit where I put on my shoes and start walking down to Deboche.

Strolling through the dense rhododendron forest, in the fading light, I come across Kumar. He is on his way up towards Tengboche. He reminds me of a little leprechaun, with his pixy hat and pinched features. We exchange a few words. He didn't know I had shifted to Deboche. Apparently he had taken some supplies to a lodge further up the valley as a favour to the owner of Trekkers Lodge, and now he is owed some money and free food. I had wanted a porter who was as unobtrusive as possible and Kumar is definitely working diligently on the concept.

"What time you leave Deboche tomorrow?" he asks.

"Nine o'clock," I tell him.

"I come before nine o'clock," he promises.

I am no longer the only trekker at Mingma's lodge. Three Western men sit in the dining room including a Talkative Climber who speaks loudly and virtually non-stop. He wears gaiters and a scarf wrapped over his head, pirate fashion as he gives a monologue about his climbing experiences.

"You should have seen it," he says, loudly. "The snow was this deep." He lifts his hand to show us how deep the snow was.

Last night, I was disappointed because the only trekker at the lodge wouldn't say a word to me, not even *bonjour*. Tonight, we have this loquacious chatterbox. I've been spoilt. I had the lodge to myself this morning and now I don't want to share it. Preferring to eat in the kitchen, I find Santos cooking at his post by the stove. On one of the burners is a three-tiered array of brass pots to distil *rakshi*, the local alcohol. He gives me a glass of milk tea.

"No charge," he tells me, generously, although it is not actually his tea to give away, so his munificence is misleading.

One of the three trekkers comes into the kitchen from the dining room and asks for a pizza with a double serving of yak cheese. Mingma is just behind him.

"*Nak* cheese," Mingma corrects him.

"*Nak* cheese?" the trekker repeats.

"Yaks are males, and *naks* are the females," Mingma explains. "I've never heard of a male yak giving milk for cheese." He says this with a tone of sarcasm.

"But everybody calls it yak cheese," the Westerner objects.

"Everybody is wrong," Mingma replies, straight-faced.

"What's the difference between a *zopkio* and a *zum*?" I ask, when the trekker leaves. It's a burning question I've been thinking about for days.

"They are both offspring from a yak and a cow, but the *zopkio* is an ox, the *zum* is a female," Mingma says.

"And the *zum* can give milk?" Mingma nods. "So we could be eating *nak* cheese or *zum* cheese?" I ask.

"Or cow cheese, or buffalo cheese, or even goat cheese," Mingma adds, smiling. He offers me a boiled potato from a bowl full of steaming potatoes. I eat the skin of my potato while he carefully peels his. "We have fifteen different kind of potatoes in this area," he adds. "Some are sweet, some small, some round, some red but we always peel them. Sherpas are experts of potatoes, even if we don't eat the skin."

Mingma has two children, both at English boarding school in Kathmandu. Sitting with him is a female helper. I'm not quite sure what their relationship is. And there is a younger, fresh-faced Sherpa woman who is the lodge owner's second wife. The owner, a director of Wilderness Travel in Kathmandu, is divorced and now has this pretty young woman as his second wife, up here on a visit.

"How much do you pay rent here?" I ask Mingmo, after the owner's wife leaves.

"Five hundred thousand rupees rent per year." That's about seven thousand dollars. "Plus, I have to also pay electricity, local porters to fetch water, my staff, porters to carry supplies from Jiri or Lukla or Namche."

"And the pony I saw outside earlier?" I ask. "Is it yours?"

"My Mercedes," he laughs. "I rent it to tourists who have altitude sickness, to get them to Namche. Only one hundred and fifty dollars. Although it is a Mercedes, it costs less than a helicopter." He laughs again at his own joke. "Mostly Japanese are using my Mercedes because they go too fast up the valley because they do not have enough holiday time away from work." Just the thought of this and he breaks into a laughing fit. "Japanese people are like eggs. If you drop them, or squeeze them, suddenly they are finished."

"And the Nepalese people, what are they like?" I ask.

Mingma thinks a while then, with a broad smile, he says, "Nepalese people are like potatoes. Drop them, squeeze them, no problem. They are still potatoes." And he laughs even harder at the appropriate description.

I remember at a British Army boarding school in Singapore, when I was fifteen; there were several Nepalese boys at the school, the sons of Ghurkha officers. One of them was my best friend, Jhalak Rai. Fed three meals a day, he had thighs the size of my chest. In fact, all the Nepalese boys thrived on the nutritious food and were stars of the school rugby team. With their cartoon Hulk-like physiques, they were invincible.

Santos makes pizza, *momos*, and a vegetable omelette for the three trekkers in the dining room. There is a colossal use of wood for the fireplace as he chucks a couple more logs in the fire to stoke up the flames.

Mingma insists that I drink some of his *rakshi*. I take the proffered glass. When I ask him why he isn't drinking he replies, "I drank too much last night with some friends." I look at the unidentified Nepalese woman sitting with us. "This is my sister," Mingma introduces her. "She is twenty-five and does not want to get married, except to an Englishman who is healthy and wealthy." Mingma clarifies, "But no Nepalese."

One of the three trekkers comes into the kitchen and asks how much the rooms cost. Mingma tells him. "That's more expensive than Namche," the trekker complains, but Mingma only shrugs. "What are you drinking?" the trekker asks me, staring at the glass of clear liquid.

"*Rakshi*, it's locally brewed alcohol," Mingma replies on my behalf, and proffers a glass. The trekker declines. "No charge,"

Mingma offers generously as he picks up the bowl full of boiled potatoes covered in *nak* cheese. "Have one. No charge for this either."

The trekker helps himself, and then returns to the climber's monologue in the dining room.

Santos cooks and serves everyone dinner and then, in a scene straight out of Charles Dicken's *Oliver Twist*, sits on a stool by the fire and helps himself to whatever food scraps are left. Occasionally, he looks at me from under the baseball cap he wears, and flashes the same broad smile. He could be the Artful Dodger. I saw him earlier in the day, on his knees scrubbing the wooden floorboards in the kitchen. The place is spotless, quite unlike the lodges at Tengboche.

An animated dialogue takes place now between Santos and Mingma. I understand little as the discussion becomes heated. Frustrated, I ask Mingma what they are talking about.

"We are discussing our different cultures," he replies. "Santos is a Rai and Hindu and a little bit Buddhist, with some local beliefs. The porter who carried your pack this morning is a Chetri and Hindu. We are Sherpas and Buddhist. We are comparing our cultures."

Again, they become embroiled in their discussion so I leave to check my laundry on the clothesline above the iron stove in the dining room. Unbelievably, the Talkative Climber is still going on about his climbing and travel experiences.

"Ach, Afghanistan is beautiful, huh. But Iran? My God, that is really beautiful, but dangerous. Kashmir is nice too."

My clothes seem dry, even Kevin's heavy cotton shirt. I pull the garments off the line, bundle them in my arms. Before turning in for the night, I go outside for a last pee. The moon is still hidden behind Ama Dablam's intimidating silhouette but above, Thamserku is bathed in the moonlight. The sky has cleared. I wonder if the four climbers are awake and what they can see from their tiny tent on the ledge below the summit. Are we just a few twinkling lights down here below the clouds? These minutes alone, standing outside looking at the Himalayan mountains with its backdrop of sky, feeling the crisp freshness of the air, listening to the dull roar of the river in the valley below, are the highlights of my trips to these mountains

When I begin to shiver I go to my narrow room, separated from the others by thin planks loosely fitted together. Once I slide into my sleeping bag on the tiny wooden bed, I dig out my wax earplugs from my backpack. It's that, or else I'll be subject to the Talkative Climber's monologue in the dining room. Of course he could be a brilliant climber, but in my limited experience, the really good climbers are rather modest and circumspect in describing their climbing prowess. But what did Laxmi tell me in her pique, describing her ex-fiancé? "Climbers have big mouths and even bigger egos." Just before I squash the earplug in place, I hear the Talkative Climber's words, booming through the thin walls.

"In the high mountains, on the pass, I had my gaiters on, but anyway snow came over my boots, the snow was so deep..."

I lift the hood of my mummy sleeping bag around my head, and pull the cord tight.

10

Deboche-Pheriche
The Doctor's Camp

My own coughing wakes me up. First it is a tickle in the throat, and then, once the coughing starts, it's hard to stop it. I get out of bed, get dressed, and head for the kitchen. Already the stove is blazing and Santos is hard at work. He seems to be the only one awake. I sit close to the warm stove and ask for a *nak* cheese omelette.

"You want chapatti?" Santos asks.

"Please." Chapatti is a simple flatbread but it takes practice to make it right. I also order a small pot of milk tea and watch as Santos fetches a cup and serves it to me. I hold the cup in both hands as the steam rises into my face.

"This from me," he says, as he fetches another thermos of milk tea. He gets on with making my omelette and the chapatti. I am amazed at how quickly he works. Because he is so small, he looks much younger than he is. His baseball cap is cocked at a rakish angle, which only serves to enhance his Artful Dodger smile. Within minutes the *nak* cheese omelette is ready. He serves it to me, but when he flips the chapatti over, he's not happy.

"Oh, chapatti no good. Don't jump."

"Don't jump?" I ask. I stand up to look at this chapatti that won't jump before realizing what he means. It hasn't risen. "No problem, I'll eat it anyway." I grab an edge of the hot chapatti and drop it on my plate with the half-eaten omelette.

Mingma's sister walks in. She takes a quick look at my plate. "Chapatti is no good?"

"It didn't rise," I reply. "Santos tried to tell me the chapatti didn't jump. Can you explain to him that in English, chapattis don't *jump*, they *rise*."

She tells him, and he understands immediately. The sister looks at me.

"Only monkeys jump," she says.

Santos smiles, and adds, "Only monkeys jump, and I."

We all laugh together at his joke. Santos grabs a towel hanging from a nail and wipes his sweaty face on it. It's the same towel he used to soak up the surplus fat and oil from the surface of the omelette he just served me.

A guide from a passing trekking group comes into the kitchen and asks to use Mingma's phone. He wants to book ahead at a lodge in Namche. When Kumar arrives, I pack my things, pay my bill and leave Santos a substantial tip. Outside it's grey, almost black with storm clouds hiding the mountains. There's no doubt now that the four climbers will have to remain holed up inside that little orange tent on the ledge below the summit of Ama Dablam. The blizzard will surely pen them in and they'll be unable to move until the weather changes.

Almost as soon as Kumar and I start walking, it begins to snow. There is a grey, depressing feel to the day, emphasised by the falling snowflakes. The wet flakes splat against the hard ground, a harbinger of what is to come. We are soon confronted with armies of Nepalese porters carrying supplies out of the mountains. There is a lingering smell of smoke and grease as they pass by. Their trekker clients come hurtling down the trail, escaping the bad weather that's setting in. It's not an encouraging prospect, heading into mountains that are black with snow clouds. Many of the trekkers coming down wear gaiters, an indication that there is deep snow at higher levels. I'm in these mountains so late in the season because I couldn't have managed any earlier with my damaged back, and I'm pushing the limits as it is. But also because I've always preferred coming into the mountains late in the season, after the peak period of October and early November, when there are fewer foreign trekkers to share the experience with.

We meet a small boy coming up the path, and he brightens my day by showing me a wooden kaleidoscope that a tourist must have given him. He is immensely proud of his possession and skips on down the path, one eye staring through the prism.

We cross a suspension bridge over the river to the other side of the valley and then climb slowly to Pangboche. This was the highest permanently occupied village until trekkers created a demand in winter for accommodation and food further up the trail. The path threads lodges on either side of the mist-shrouded village. This collection of buildings doesn't seem a Sherpa community so much as a gauntlet of wall-to-wall lodges. Smoke rises from tin-can smokestacks. Through the windows I see a few trekkers inside huddled against the cold. Although I had intended to stop in Pangboche, no lodge is sufficiently alluring to entice me in. I keep walking and Kumar, perhaps a little chagrined at my reprimand for yesterday's disappearing act, sticks with me.

The countryside is desolate and the day is overcast with storms high above, and mist swilling about at ground level. The scenery is monochromatic: everything, from the mountains to the ground, is either snow white, darkish black, or grey. There are no trees and the scrubs and bushes are barely noticeable in this gargantuan landscape. It's a surreal environment, not fit for human habitation, and yet here I am heading into it in December, and an oncoming snowstorm. A porter descends, carrying a woman trekker in a bamboo basket on his back. The rest of her group walk quietly in single file behind their guides. I look down the valley to where I have just come from. It's not an inspiring sight, not like the last couple of days when the sun was shining warm on the skin, and the river sparkled in its bright light. Heading up the valley, I pass several isolated lodges, their windows and doors locked for the season. Ahead is yet another *chorten* erected to the memory of a dead climber.

> *Memory of*
> *Michael Knakkergaard Jorgensen*
> *Denmark.*
> *Makalu Expedition*
> *4/30/98*

Joergensen, a highly respected guide and climber, was the first Dane to summit Everest, in 1995. Well-liked and considered a very safe climber, he was the leader of the eight-member Makalu International Expedition. After reaching the summit of Makalu, on the Tibet side, Joergensen died on the descent, when his rope broke. He fell 500 feet to his death.

I stand for a few minutes to pay my respect. All of this, the snowstorm, the closed and locked lodges, the greyness of the day, seem to be omens now. But I keep on, passing over a windswept ridge before I descend, gradually, down towards Pheriche, which is barely discernible through the mist. Pheriche is mostly just a flat stretch of ground between the stream and a higher ridge separating the Khumbu and Lhotse/Imja valleys. Its emptiness is broken only by stone-walled yak enclosures, and a few low stone buildings. On a wide wooden bridge cantilevered over the rushing stream, a tightly knit group of trekkers push by me. They look miserable, as if desperate to get out of there. There can't be a metre separating one from the other as they are led by young, good-looking Sherpa guides fashionable in the latest mountain clothing.

Kumar follows me at a discrete distance as I struggle up the footpath through Pheriche. The place looks abandoned. The first lodges I walk by are shuttered and locked up. Deep snowdrifts have accumulated against the north-facing walls. I continue until I see the sign for the Himalayan Rescue Association. The door is closed and a notice outside says *Gone to Lunch*. It is too cold and dismal to wait, so I proceed to the nearest lodge, twenty metres away. A woman milking a *nak* outside sees me looking through the window.

"You stay here?" she asks, and pushes the door open for me. She is barely discernible from the gloom inside because her face and hands are dark with grime. The interior of the lodge is shabby and filthy.

"Maybe," I tell her. I'll decide after I have eaten.

She takes my request for vegetable soup and disappears into the kitchen. In the meantime, two young boys and a little girl come out of the kitchen. They each have parallel lines of bright yellow snot hanging from their nostrils. They play inside for a while before going out to the courtyard. I watch them through the window. Both boys wear trousers with wide splits up the backside. When one of the boys squats, the slit at the back automatically opens. A smile on his face, he calmly excretes a lump of shit into the dirt. The other boy looks at it, then picks it up and throws it away. All three children scamper back into the kitchen where my lunch is being made.

I will find another lodge.

When the HRA offices open, I step inside, to what is both the waiting room and the consultation room. A young Nepalese porter is complaining of dizziness, but the dizziness has gone he says. The doctor, a Canadian, looks him over but there is little she can do for him now. He smiles, as if pleased to have her attention. And no wonder, the doctor is gorgeous, a tall and slim young woman with full lips and dark hair. I notice that her long fingers are scarred, as if they have scaled many rock faces. She's obviously a serious climber. She asks the porter if there is anything else wrong. He says he has an earache. Her Nepalese assistant translates this for the doctor.

"How long has he had the earache?" the doctor asks.

The question is relayed to the porter, and the answer given back.

"For some years."

The doctor gives him a tube of ointment and charges him a handful of rupees. The porter pulls out the Nepalese rupees from his jean pockets and leaves, happy to have been treated.

The next patient is a large Sherpa woman, as well built as a man, wearing a traditional Sherpa robe and colourful apron. Her hair is tied in pigtails. The doctor asks her where she lives. This surprises me because there can't be that many people living in Pheriche, and this wealthy Sherpa woman owns the largest lodge, barely fifty metres away. I had seen the woman outside her lodge, on the pathway through Pheriche. I wonder how the doctor can have been so isolated during her two-month stay here not to have encountered her neighbour.

The woman's ailment is a persistent cough. She is checked over by the doctor. When asked to pay the subsidized Nepalese rate for the appointment, she pulls out a couple of tatty rupee notes. She does not have enough money to pay the full fee, but then she smiles, displaying a front gold tooth. She gets away with tight-fistedness. While the poor Nepalese porter paid the fee in full, the relatively wealthy Sherpa lodge-owner wheedled her way out of paying a few rupees.

Next in line is a Sherpa guide who tells the doctor that he has two Japanese clients who are constipated.

"They should be so lucky," the doctor comments. "Where are they?"

"In their tents," the guide replies.

"Well, tell them to come here if they want treatment," she says. "I'm sure they can walk the short distance. And if they're constipated it will probably do them some good."

The guide leaves to relay the message to his clients, and I'm next in line.

"I've had this persistent cough," I tell the doctor, although it's probably unnecessary. I've been hacking and coughing since I walked in. "I've had it since I arrived in Lukla, about a week ago." She hands me a bottle of cough syrup.

"That should calm it down and let you get some sleep at night," she says. "Five hundred rupees." Seven dollars! More than ten times what the Nepalese patients were charged, but it's one way to subsidize the clinic. And the clinic provides health facilities for local people, as well as the trekkers who pass through.

"Have you had many serious cases of altitude sickness?" I ask.

"Almost thirty helicopter evacuations in the time I've been here," she says. "That's one almost every other day, on average. I've seen about four hundred patients in the same time. Normally, we'd be gone by now, but we decided to stay an extra couple of days. We're leaving day after tomorrow."

Outside it is bitterly cold and a fierce wind blows down the valley, over the desolate hamlet that is Pheriche. Historically, these rough stone huts, mostly owned by villagers from Khunde, would have sheltered the yak herders who brought their yak up here during the summer months.

At three in the afternoon, the doctor gives her daily talk on high altitude sickness at the newly constructed solarium outside the HRA building. The solarium works fine when there's bright sunlight. Without the sun, the cold wind whistles through the gaps between the glass panes, and the rough-hewn planks of wood. There are only eight of us attending the session, including three of the British army soldiers that Christina has been accompanying. One of the soldiers has problems adjusting to the altitude and is there for an appointment with the doctor. He tells me that Christina has been looking for me, that she's with the rest of their group in Dingboche.

"Are you heading there tonight?" I ask. I'm tempted to walk over there myself, take another day to acclimatize to the altitude.

"No, we're not trained to go over the snowline," another soldier replies. He sees the perplexed look on my face. "To get to Dingboche, we'd have to climb over the ridge and there's snow up there."

I look through the dirty windows at the ridge, no more than two hundred metres higher, separating Pheriche from Dingboche. I guess there was no snow when they arrived here.

"But it's only a half-hour walk and there's hardly any snow."

"Those are the rules," the soldier days. "If we haven't been trained to walk in snow, we can't cross the ridge. We have to go all the way around and if we did, it would be nightfall by then."

"And you're not trained to walk at night either?" I ask, not intending to sound supercilious. He doesn't answer my question. The British Army uses these mountains to train its soldiers but it sometimes seems the professional soldiers are wetter behind the ears than the trekkers wandering around up here.

Outside, it's snowing harder. Snow billows off the peaks like active volcanoes spewing black smoke. The mountains look powerful and angry, and I definitely wouldn't want to be up there. I wonder if the four Ama Dablam climbers are still in their tent. There is no way of knowing. The swirling clouds render even the shoulders of the immense mountains invisible. Without the tops of the mountains to distract the eye with their spectacular presence, the eyes tend to focus on ground level. Devoid of direct sunlight to provide some brightness to the landscape, it becomes stark, harsh, and dreary.

I make for the largest lodge in Pheriche, the one owned by the Sherpa woman who had just visited the clinic. She is holding court in the kitchen. The lodge seems to be empty until I hear the three British soldiers in the dining room. I stay in the kitchen and write down my order in a ledger book with my room number scrawled on the cover. A young Sherpa girl, obviously the Sherpa woman's daughter, busily prepares the food on a kerosene stove. Kumar drops my pack in my single room and disappears. I know he has gone to one of the smaller lodges, where he is comfortable, and where he will soon be helping to peel vegetables, fetch water, and assist in whatever chores need to be done. In larger lodges like this, he is not so welcome, and so he does not feel at ease.

Yangtze Sherpa's daughter Tzangpo, serves me Sherpa stew, a mixture of vegetables, potatoes, rice and lots of garlic. Having loaded up on carbohydrates, I head back into the storm to wander through the settlement in the direction of Everest. Already it's almost dark, and in the semi-gloom I see several yak calmly chewing their cuds in a nearby pasture. I notice another lonely trekker, wandering around by himself, absent-mindedly kicking pebbles in the path.

When it is almost too dark to see any longer, I return to the lodge and sit with several Nepalese around the space heater in the dining room. Several porters are hunched together as they flip through the pages of a woman's magazine, giggling at the photographs of semi-clad women. Although not titillating to a desensitised Western man, the ads showing women in underwear are stimulating enough for the Rai boys.

In the kitchen, two well-dressed young Sherpa men remain aloof from the snickering Rai porters. They both have long hair with Oakley sunglasses holding their groomed manes in place. They wear jeans, and one has a Ralph Lauren polo shirt and sheepskin-lined suede booties. The way they sit, their body language, is so different from that of the porters. Finally, one of them says to me, "Where you from?" in a perfect American accent.

"You'd never guess," I reply.

"Bermuda," he says, and I'm stunned.

"How'd you know?" I ask.

"I'm psychic." He sees the look of disbelief on my face. "I met someone else from Bermuda, and he also told me I'd never guess where he's from."

He then tells me he is Tzangpo's younger brother, and the older man next to him is her husband. He is sophisticated and cool. A university student in Kathmandu, his family are from Khunde. His grandfather brought their yak up here to graze during the summers when he was a boy. Now they have a house in Kathmandu, a restaurant in Thamel, an export business, and another lodge in Dingboche, which they rent out. They are, in a word, rich. They are rich not only by Nepalese standards, but by Western standards as well. From the information he tells me about the number of guests staying there, I calculate that this lodge alone must make, during the peak season of three months, over one hundred thousand dollars.

To these elite Sherpas, I am an individual trekker and of no particular significance or interest. The brother starts a conversation with Tzangpo's husband, so I head off to bed.

Still fighting altitude headaches at night, I have a daily conflict of interest. On the one hand, it's important to keep drinking copious amounts of water to help avoid altitude sickness. On the other hand, I hate getting up during the night with a full bladder and having to go outside into the freezing dark for a pee. Because I have a warm sleeping bag, I go to bed at night wearing only my underpants, even up here in the mountains. I keep a pair of flip-flops on the floor beside my bed so that I can slip into them easily, minimising the time I am out of the warm sleeping bag.

As usual, within hours of falling asleep, I wake up with a bladder about to burst. I slip out of my triple-layer sleeping bag, feel around with my toes for the flip-flops, put them on, search for the latch on the door, open it, and then with outstretched hands grope along the dark corridor to the exterior door. When I step outside, it is surprisingly bright and I think it must be a full moon. But when I look down at the ground, I can't see my shadow. I reach down and touch the ground and realize why it's so bright. It's covered in centimetres of snow. I cross the footpath and step through the gate, towards the outdoor toilet. I have no intention of stumbling all the way there just for a pee when a snow bank in the enclosure will do as well. Hooking my underpants down with my thumb, I am about to urinate when I hear a grunt that sounds very much like a bear. Turning, I spot the unmistakable image of a lunging brown grizzly. I turn and run, my flip-flops slipping on the snowy ground. A brief glance over my shoulder and I'm certain it's a grizzly chasing me. I manage to punch open the wooden door to the ramshackle drop toilet and slam it shut before the animal is upon me.

I lean with my back against the cubicle door, breathing hard. Somewhere within the dark confines of this little space is an undefined hole in the ground over a pyramid of excrement. I'm not sure which would be worse, plunging down the hole or being ripped apart by a bear. With the sudden physical and mental exertion my altitude headache returns with a vengeance. Ignoring my pounding head and thumping heart, I slowly take my weight off the door. I can hear the animal outside, and its vigorous breathing. But its footsteps, as it circles the toilet, sound more like cloven hooves than the padded paws of a bear. Besides, I realise as I take stock of the situation, there aren't any grizzlies in the Himalayans, are there? And whatever indigenous bears they do have must be as rare as rocking-horse manure. Blindly avoiding the centre of the cubicle where the drop must be, I step ever so carefully around the edges of the cubicle and look through the glass window at the back. I can see the hairy profile of an enormous brown-haired yak circling the toilet, searching for me. This one has no horns, and with its humped back and shaggy appearance, it looks exactly like a grizzly, especially on a dark night like this. And it grunts.

It's several degrees below zero, and I'm standing outside in underpants and flip-flops, shivering uncontrollably. If I don't get out of the toilet soon, I won't have to worry about being mauled by a grizzly or a yak, or the consequences of dropping into the cavity below the fragile floorboards. I'm going to slowly freeze to death. While there's no shame freezing to death while climbing Everest, there's every disgrace in freezing to death in flip-flops and underpants, inside a crappy outhouse, trapped by a hornless yak.

Peering through cracks in the door, I see a stone wall right in front of the toilet. I calculate the distance, fling open the door, and bolt for the wall. My flip-flops slither on the snow-covered stones but I manage to claw my way over the wall, and then drop to the ground on the other side. I get up and make a mad dash for the opening in the enclosure, then up the footpath and back to the lodge, before the yak has figured it out.

Back in my room I shut and bolt the door, then brush away the snow and strip off my wet underpants. Panting from the exertion and fright, I lie back on my sleeping bag. I promise myself that in the future, I'll sleep in thermal underwear, just in case another belligerent yak catches me having a pee in the middle of the night.

As I lay there wheezing in the freezing dark I just pray no one saw my ridiculous escapade.

⚜

11

Pheriche-Dingboche Backtracking

At breakfast I meet a trekker, an American who has already spent three months trekking around Nepal. He sits huddled against the cold, the hood to his sweatshirt pulled over his head so that only his face is visible. Several days' growth of a grey beard makes him look older than he is. He strikes me as another one of "the lost", searching for his true self among the ice and crevices of the Himalayas. His spectacles steam up as he sips a mug of hot tea. Every breath of each sentence sounds like his last dying gasp.

"Going up to Gorak Shep, or down?" I ask. I now have the savvy now to say "Gorak Shep" rather than "Everest Base Camp". Hardly any trekkers go to the modern Everest Base Camp, although most of us attempt to get to the old Everest Base Camp, Gorak Shep, at five thousand one hundred and seventy metres. Once there, most of us want to climb further, up the hump called Kala Pattar, at five thousand six hundred metres, another five hundred metres higher.

The trekker is going down, and can hardly wait to get out of these mountains.

"I'm sick of the food," he says. "And if I have to inhale this yak shit smoke any more, I'm going to be seriously ill." He says this just as a porter carries a handful of dried yak dung to fuel the space heater.

Tzangpo's brother wears a pony-tail this morning. His only role in the lodge seems to be tallying up the bills. As I pay, I glance over my shoulder, to make sure no one is there to hear what I'm about to ask. The lodge is mostly empty, the British soldiers still sleeping.

"Does your brown yak, the one in the enclosure outside where the toilet is, does he tend to chase people?" I ask.

"He does it all the time," the Sherpa replies flicking his hair casually over his shoulder.

Kumar shows up, eager and ready to go.

"Up to now," I tell him, "I've been choosing which village we go to. Today you choose." Kumar smiles. For the first time, he's wearing windproof pants and proper hiking boots.

"Dingboche," he says. This is a half-hour detour up an adjacent side valley and not in the direction of Everest, which will mean adding to the length of the trip and his term of employment with me.

"Okay," I say, "And you choose the lodge too," I add. I'm curious to see where he takes me.

"Okay," he says, smiling happily.

The day is brighter than yesterday, but the mountains are still concealed behind boiling clouds that streak off knife-sharp ridges. Nevertheless, it seems more cheerful today, probably because there is snow on the ground everywhere, a reminder of Christmas, which isn't far off. The snow brightens the landscape, disguising the dark, stark rock. I try to imagine what the British soldiers will do today if they are not authorised to walk in snow, because there is snow everywhere. They won't be able to put a foot out of the lodge. Maybe that's why they haven't bothered getting out of bed. Seems to defeat the whole purpose in sending these soldiers up here to harden them up and get them used to high altitude and the cold when they aren't allowed to do anything that might jeopardize their health. Suddenly, just as I am thinking all this, there's a loud crack of an avalanche somewhere in the distance. The first loud retort is succeeded by several more. Hmm, maybe the British soldiers' commanding officers have a point.

In patches of blue sky, slats of snow fall brightly in the sunlight. In other places they are grey sheets under the backdrop of dark black clouds. Hundreds of yellow-billed choughs play in the thermals rising off the crest separating the two valleys. It's a magical sight. From the top of the ridge I have a view down the valley towards Tengboche, and up the two valleys, towards Everest Base

Camp on one side and Chukhung on the other. The despondent mood I felt yesterday dissipates as the scraps of blue sky grow larger and the blanket of snow underfoot begins to melt in the warm sunlight. The path towards Dingboche passes numerous *chortens* and *mani* walls and prayer flags fluttering from prominent edges. Thin veils of mist in the lower recesses of the valley hang as stationary as if they were a watercolour painting. By contrast, the jet stream blows clouds spilling off Ama Dablam and Thamserku. The windward sides of both mountains are relatively clear, while the leeward sides are constantly changing kaleidoscopes of roiling black clouds.

The cries of alpine choughs are interrupted by the repeated crack of avalanches tumbling unseen down mountainsides. As the snow melts and the air warms in the sunlight, there's a pervasive smell of damp yak dung. Several huge shaggy yak with hair that reaches the ground and great bushy tails, graze on the slopes overlooking Dingboche. Looking like grizzly bears in the middle of the night, they more closely resemble bison during the day, with their massive shoulder humps. I have carried a wooden stick since Lukla and I keep it cocked and ready to swing at any yak that stares at me too long.

Dingboche, as the guidebooks advise, is not as windy or as exposed as Pheriche and it more closely resembles a genuine Sherpa yak herders community, rather than being dominated by lodges. From the vantage point of the ridge it's amazing how Dingboche melts into the landscape. All the round boulders forming the walls of the *chhusas*, and yak herders' huts blend in perfectly with their rocky surrounds.

Kumar chooses a lodge of his own liking. The owner and her staff in the kitchen are decidedly friendly, although the mishmash of electrical wires hanging off the walls make me wonder how long the structure will last before something short-circuits and the wooden building burns to the ground. Several certificates hang on the dining room wall. One admits Sonahishi Sherpa as a member of the National Geographic Society. There is a photograph of the owner of the lodge, apparently a high altitude climber, with Jimmy Carter and his wife. There is a letter from Mountain Travel certifying that Sonam attended the Palisade School of Mountaineering. On a more mundane level is a certificate of

Training for Lodge Owners. The owner's wife leads me to the penthouse suite, an upper room with glass windows on all four sides. The lodge is empty, and although there are four beds, she promises me I'll be the only one in the room, for a hundred rupees, or a buck-fifty.

The sun emerges and steam rises off the enclosed potato fields as snow melts. Rather than hang around the lodge all day, I go for a walk back up the ridge where there is a *gompa* built into the rock cliff face. I follow yak paths zigzagging up the steep hill but have to stop frequently to catch my breath. Several times I come across a yak lying on the ground sleepily chewing its cud. On a relatively flat patch I see a dozen yak, or *nak*, it's impossible to tell which, with their shaggy stomachs and bushy tails hiding any obvious gender differences. Two of them cough a deep-seated cough that shakes their whole ribcage. They stick their tongues out, as if provoking each other. The two coughing yak are bigger than the others and when they both arch their hairy tails over their backs, exposing their genitals, I guess they must be males. They rub their foreheads into bushes and exposed rocks. One shakes himself and a cloud of brown dust comes off his course hide like a dirty carpet beaten with a switch. And then, suddenly, one charges the other and they start fighting.

I scramble out of the way in case they lose their focus and decide to pick on me instead. From a small stream I fill my water bottle for the third time today and drop an iodine tablet into the bottle. So far, despite the annoying cough and headaches, I haven't been sick. Higher up, the Alpine choughs play, hundreds upon hundreds of them. I've found that where the choughs play is often the most spiritually fulfilling spot to sit and contemplate. When they ride the thermals, their wings extend, and their tails twist and turn as they bank and surf the invisible currents of air like gliders. But when they dive, they remind me of fighter jets with sweptback wings as they go whistling by. There doesn't seem to be any manoeuvre they would be incapable of, and most of the flying seems to have no motive. It's as if they fly for fun. I can't see why else they would perform these acrobatics if it weren't for the sheer exhilaration of it. Lost in my own world and absentmindedly following the path, I almost walk into a brown yak with a loop of rope through its nose. I take the telltale rope as an indication that he may have a bad temper. I back up and give him a wide berth. A trekker was killed here last year by a yak, and I don't want to contribute to this year's statistics.

Small blue flowers grow close to the ground. Are they Edelweiss or gentian? I contour the mountainside into the upper reaches of the valley, past a *mani* wall towards a hermitage sealed with antique locks. On the small courtyard area in front of the dwelling I watch the clouds and birds while trying to ignore a throbbing altitude headache. Then I reach for my zippered back pocket to make sure the envelope is still there. It is.

Could this... be the place?

It doesn't feel right. Not friendly enough, and the shut hermitage, even if it has only been abandoned for the winter, doesn't add any spiritual energy to the place.

Recovering from my headache, I walk back down to my lodge in Dingboche where I wash my hair in a basin of hot water in the courtyard. Relatively spruced up, I relax with my back to the sun drenched wall of the kitchen and read a book in the warmth of the sun. A camping group arrives, comprised of only half-a-dozen clients, including Jackie, the doctor I met briefly at the Khunde hospital. She is with the group to cater to any medical emergencies, in addition to a retinue of Nepalese staff that must exceed thirty members, not including four yaks. The clients are patently wealthy, including a tall American patriarch with two statuesque, pretty daughters in their mid-twenties. As I watch them settle in, it becomes clear the two daughters are fed up of sleeping on the cold ground in tents. They seem to have mutinied. Although their tents are neatly erected with military precision in the field opposite, the daughters are staying in the lodge.

Because I was the first one here this morning, and because the owner promised me that I could have the room to myself, I retain the "honeymoon suite". At least, this is what one of the daughters called it after climbing the stairs to inspect my room through the pane glass windows. For a moment, I fear I'll be petitioned to give it over to them. In no time, the girls are in a heated argument over who will take the first shower.

The others seem to have united behind the daughters in their dissension against the uncomfortable living standards of the tents. The unhappy group sits in the glass sunroom eating soup. I sit in the sunlight, pretending to read my book, but keenly eavesdropping and observing. The Tall Patriarch oozes power and authority and money and it's fascinating to watch him in action.

The Sherpa *sirdar* is equally interesting. He treats the porters, the lodge owner, me, with disdain, as if deliberately cultivating the arrogant attitude of his client. He struts around with a baseball cap on his head, a thick down jacket, one hand behind his back and the other holding a toothpick in the corner of his mouth, under a neatly trimmed moustache. But when he talks to the Tall Patriarch, he is deferential to the point of being obsequious. He removes his baseball cap, and the toothpick, and stoops slightly instead of prancing around like a puffed-up pigeon. He grovels about his benefactor, offering cups of tea, biscuits, warm down jacket, anything to please the great man. Between grovelling sessions, he tells the Tall Patriarch how he needs money to build a lodge in Namche. From the conversation, I gather the Tall Patriarch owns a chain of hotels in Hawaii and has already sponsored his fawning guide with an eighteen-month hotel training programme. Now his Sherpa guide is angling for another work-study stint in Hawaii, to raise more money for his lodge.

A Sherpa woman in a long grey dress and a colourful apron carries buckets of hot water to the wooden shack that is the shower. She is in stark contrast to the two long-legged sisters who are almost as tall as their father. Although the Americans have asked for a hot shower, the two women look spotlessly clean already. The Sherpa woman is grimy and probably hasn't had a shower in a long time. Probably about the same age as the two American women, mid-twenties, she could pass for being a decade older. She is short and thickset, although pretty. She watches enviously, bucket in hand, as the first of the two daughters strides into the cubicle with an armful of shampoos, soaps, lotions and perfumes.

"Where can I get a Coke?" the other daughter asks the Sherpa woman. "I feel like a Coke."

The Sherpa woman fetches a Coke and the daughter asks her father to pay for it.

"It's three dollars for a Coke," he laughs, "and only a dollar for a room. Where else in the world would you pay three times the cost of a hotel room for a Coke?"

Or perhaps more appropriately, a hotel room for a third of the cost of a Coke.

The first daughter comes out of the shower cubicle, with long wet hair wrapped up in a towel, turban style. The second daughter steps in, as the Sherpa woman carries more buckets of steaming hot water and pours it in the container above the shower stall.

As the sun sets high on the mountains amidst a flurry of clouds, a delicate white mist drifts slowly up the valley. With all the yaks wandering around Dingboche, I don't want to repeat last night's Keystone Cops escapade. I ask the Sherpa woman if she has an empty water bottle. She fetches one from the kitchen. In my room, I take out my Swiss army knife and cut off the top and begin my nightly ritual of laying out all the things I need around the top end of my sleeping bag so I can easily find them when I wake up in the middle of the night. The empty pee bottle I place on the floorboards near my bed.

From my penthouse suite, I have a panoramic view of the mountains. The cheap Chinese sheets on all four beds have been turned down, neatly folding over at the corner, just as you might expect in a five star hotel. The sun disappears as the heavy mist glides past. I have time to take one quick photo of a sunset-lit Lhotse, protruding through an opening, before we are enveloped in the silent, damp embrace of thick mist.

In the dining room, the Tall Patriarch asks, noticing me for the first time.

"You going up or down?" he asks.

"Up," I reply.

"Oh," he says. Having no status at all, he looks right through me. I should have lied, told him I was on my way down, and made up all kinds of stories of what it's like "up there". I could have mimicked the Talkative Climber, regaled them all with stories of how deep the snow was, an ice pick in each of my hands to punctuate my sentences for emphasis.

The British doctor Jackie sits next to me in the dining room.

"We started off camping in tents," she whispers. "They didn't like that. I can't blame them. Last night they slept in a lodge. Now they not only want to sleep in a lodge, they want to eat in the lodge as well. We started off with fifty staff for this small group of six. They've sent twenty staff back already and the other thirty have the day off because there's nothing for them to do if we eat in here. Most of the porters and kitchen staff are perfectly drunk right now."

"How do you order food?" the Tall Patriarch asks.

"Just write your order in the book corresponding to your room number," Jackie tells him.

"I'd give anything for a salad bar right now," one of the daughters says.

"Stick with me," her father advises his daughters, ignoring the last comment. "I'll take you to a lot more interesting places than either of your boyfriends."

I can't tell if this is meant as a threat or an incentive.

When it grows dark outside, two solar powered electrical fluorescent lights are switched on. One of the daughters orders French fries, but a few minutes later is surprised when French toast is served to her instead.

"Potato chips," Jackie explains to her. "You've got to order potato chips not French fries."

"Where'd you get fresh tomatoes up here?" the Tall Patriarch asks, when pizzas arrive from the kitchen, topped with fresh tomatoes.

"From Namche," the Sherpa boy who serves us replies.

"They grow them in Namche?" The Patriarch asks.

"Maybe they come from Jiri, then Namche," the boy says.

"Imagine ordering pizza with fresh tomatoes that have been carried all the way up here," the Patriarch comments. He picks up a piece of meat from the gooey *nak* cheese topping. "What kind of meat is this?"

"Yak meat," the boy answers.

"Yak meat instead of pepperoni?" He looks at his daughters. "You hear that? Tell your boyfriends your dad eats pizza with yak meat topping instead of pepperoni."

During dinner, everyone in the group approaches Jackie for medication to cure hacking coughs, explosive stomachs, and overworked joints.

"I need some sleeping tablets," one client whispers to Jackie. He looks over his shoulder to see if his roommate is listening. "He complains I'm coughing all night, but he keeps me awake by peeing so loudly into his bottle at all hours. Sounds like I'm sharing my room with a horse."

I take comfort that I'm on my own in the honeymoon suite and therefore won't be kept awake by someone's hacking cough, or be embarrassed by keeping someone else awake by peeing into my bottle. By six thirty, I am so tired I head upstairs to bed. Several times before midnight, I swivel my legs over the edge of the bed and stand up in my sleeping bag. I lower it to half-mast, pick up the plastic water bottle, and relieve myself. What a luxury not having to go outside to an outhouse.

Unfortunately, I have miscalculated the capacity of my bladder and the one-litre bottle is full come midnight. I am left back at square one, feeling my way along walls, down staircases to the courtyard below, where I relieve myself against a nearby wall. I wouldn't dream of walking behind the lodge to the drop toilets out there.

12

Dingboche-Duglha

A raven's claws sliding down the corrugated roof awakes me. Lying in the comfort of my sleeping bag, I have a spectacular panoramic view as the sun bleaches the mountains white. No one else seems to be awake, so I discretely take advantage of the time alone to creep down the stairs to the courtyard below, delicately holding out in front of me a plastic water bottle full to the cut-off brim with bright yellow urine. As I tiptoe towards the back of the lodge, one of the Tall Patriarch's daughters bumps into me as she hurriedly exits her room. Startled at the sight of my bed-head, she looks at my almost full bottle and the wet splash marks on her sleeve.

"I don't believe it," she says, when she puts two and two together.

"Neither do I," I tell her truthfully.

She gives a shriek of frustration and paces off in the direction of the drop toilets as I quickly dump the half-frozen evidence.

The path through Dingboche is an ice rink. But the upside to this cold front is the sky, which is clear blue. On the outskirts of the village, climbing up the ridge, I watch two red-beaked choughs play in the wind. They seem to be identical to the yellow-beaked choughs, apart from the colour of their beaks. Maybe they are like the red-hatted and yellow-hatted Tibetan Buddhists, signifying a slight difference in spiritual bent. Maybe the red-beaked choughs like spiralling upwards on thermals while the yellow-beaked choughs prefer diving downwards to earth with their wings folded. Or perhaps the difference is even less significant. I'd swear these choughs are reincarnated humans. I suppose you'd have to be pretty good in a previous life, though, to be reincarnated as a carefree chough playing on thermals in the Himalayas.

Wandering along the path I reminisce about our eclectic childhood. My father took sixteen-millimetre film of us as we were growing up in Hong Kong, India, Kenya, Malaysia and Singapore. Because the numerous reels were so bulky and needed an old-fashioned projector, we only saw them once, as teenagers, but last Christmas my mother had all the reels transferred onto videotape. She gave each of us four children a copy and we spent Christmas watching our lives being re-enacted in jerky images. The black-and-white video copy of the 16mm film is the most vivid memory I have of the diverse life we lived as children. The recollection of those reincarnated images of us, especially of Kevin, haunts me. I watch the choughs and the inevitable question looms once again.

How can my younger brother be dead?

I catch up to a trekking group whose *sirdar*-guide reeks of alcohol, despite the early hour. Walking in tandem with him, it's impressive to listen to the Sherpa speaking perfect French. He points around him, telling his clients which peaks he has climbed. He has a bit of a paunch, certainly doesn't appear very fit, and yet I have little doubt that he's telling the truth.

Kumar leads me along the path. We cross a mostly frozen stream, and then up to Duglha, a couple of lodges huddled together, as if for warmth and protection. The British army is there, on their high altitude training exercise, with Christina.

"Where have you been?" she asks. "I looked for you at Tengboche but you disappeared."

We sit together and eat lunch with two other groups. I study a tall, handsome Sherpa guide, his long shiny black hair pulled into a ponytail tucked neatly through the back of his baseball cap. His eyes are hidden behind mirrored Oakley sunglasses. I overhear him as he requests a pretty trekker in the group to massage his neck and shoulders. He has a couple of climbing karabiners and a walkie-talkie strapped to his belt. A large gold cross hangs from a gold necklace next to another necklace with a greenstone pendant from New Zealand.

"See the girl over there?" Christina whispers to me. She indicates with her eyes a dark-haired, not-so-attractive woman sitting off to the side, talking earnestly to another guide. "She slept with the good-looking Sherpa guide with the long hair on the second night of their trip," Christina whispers. "And he hasn't paid her any attention since. In fact, he's sleeping with the girl who's massaging his neck now."

"How do you know?" I ask.

"Because we stayed at the same lodge last night and she told me," Christina replies. "She was in tears. He put the move on her the second night and she was swept up with the romance of it all." Christina shrugs before turning to look at me. "We all do that." She adds, "Get caught up with the romance of it all."

The spurned woman is clearly making every effort to ignore the antics of her former lover. His latest conquest wears tights, showing off her slim long legs.

"How do people get themselves into such messes?" I ask.

Christina looks at me again with a knowing look, "Oh, and you've never screwed up?"

We eat lunch, and although I intend to remain here for the night so as not to ascend too far, I join Christina as she continues up to Lobuche.

"It will do me good to climb high and then come back down again," I tell her as I drink a litre of iodine-flavoured water and then fill the water bottle again.

On the way up we meet Yes Yes Shelley. She has found her beloved porter, at her side like an appendage.

"I spent three days with the lama at Tengboche," she tells me excitedly.

"Was it a good experience?" I ask. I do this deliberately so that she will reply in the affirmative and I can tell Christina why I call her Yes Yes Shelley.

"Yes yes," Shelly replies, not disappointing me. "It was a very good experience. I'm staying some weeks with him at the monastery when I go back down. He just seemed to know who I was, and why I was there."

Sonam, her guide, glowers at me over his shoulder, keen to put as much distance as possible between them and me.

We say good-bye to them and keep on walking. From Duglha, the well-trodden path leads up to the ridge of the terminal moraine of the Khumbu Glacier.

"How's your back?" Christina asks, when I stop to take a breath.

"The pains I had the first three or four days seem to have gone," I tell her. "But I couldn't have done it if Kumar weren't carrying my pack." Christina is carrying a pack that looks as tall, if not as wide, as the one Kumar carries. "How are you managing to carry that?" I ask her.

'This is nothing," she says. "Have you seen the packs of some of the soldiers I'm with? Looks as if they brought their grannies in them. Part of their training, I guess."

"Any good prospects?" I ask.

"You mean romance?" She scoffs at the thought. "I've been travelling with them for almost two weeks and now that it is clear I'm not interested in any of them, despite their advances, guess what? They're all married. Never said a word about a wife for the first few days, and then it slips out when it's obvious they are going to get nowhere with me. Doesn't give us much faith in you guys."

"We're not all like that," I protest.

'Yeah, right."

At the top of the climb Christina and I say good-bye, as she continues on, catching up to the British Army.

On the crest of the hill, numerous cairns have been erected to Sherpas and foreign climbers who have died, their bodies still high up on the mountains, an integral part of the frozen landscape now. Sherpas too have had their ashes scattered there. It's a desolate spot, overshadowed by the massive terminal moraine of the Khumbu Glacier. I notice a large cairn, dedicated to American climber Scott Fischer who died in 1966, in the single deadliest tragedy in the history of the mountain, when eight climbers perished.

Fischer reached the summit of Everest on May 10, 1996, at around 3:45 PM, but had severe difficulties descending despite being accompanied by sirdar Lopsang Sherpa. When Fischer was unable to continue he persuaded Lopsang to descend alone. Lopsang had hoped to send supplemental oxygen back up to Fischer. Boukreev made several attempts to reach the climber, but was turned back due to bad weather. Around 7PM on May 11, Boukreev was finally able to reach Fischer, but it was too late, the climber died of a severe altitude sickness. The tragedy was made famous by Jon Krakauer's best-selling book *Into Thin Air*.

Walking amidst the piles of rocks stacked on top of each other as memorials to those who never made it back out of this valley, an eerie feeling sweeps over me. Perhaps it is the intimate reminder of death. I walk some distance towards Lobuche before finally turning around and heading back down the steep slope to Duglha. It's late in the day, the rush hour of traffic of trekkers is over, and there are no more climbers coming up or going down. The path is wonderfully undisturbed.

Soon after three o'clock, the sun ducks behind the mountains, creating shadows in the valley. It grows cold very quickly. Before I reach Duglha, I meet two women heading up with heavy backpacks. It's late and they are walking at a snail's pace. They won't arrive in Lobuche until well after dark. There is no one to advise them, or take care of them if something goes wrong. I ask them if they know how long it will take them to get up to Lobuche.

"Yes," one replies, a bit testily.

"We've been up there already," the other adds. "She got sick and had to be flown out by helicopter to Kathmandu. We're trying it again and not going up so fast this time."

They continue on their way. They won't get altitude sickness by going too fast, but they're going to freeze in the dark going this slow.

Kumar is waiting for me outside the lodge. He smiles, and for the first time I wonder if he is actually looking out for me, although I shouldn't be surprised. I am after all, his walking bank account. These relationships are based purely on business transactions, but they often end up in friendships. It's not surprising, the Nepalese people are easy to like and easy to get along with. The limitation in Kumar's and my ability to communicate does stymie any blossoming friendship, but that's also what I wanted this walk to be, a solitary march into the high mountains to reflect on recent events.

The lodge at Duglha is basic. A smiling boy with manic energy bounces out of the kitchen and lights the space heater by pouring kerosene over the dried yak dung. He returns to the kitchen as if he were in a race. The room fills with yak dung and kerosene smoke until the heat in the space heater is intense enough to create its own draft up the tin can chimney.

Most of the trekkers inside the lodge are suffering, including the female half of a young couple who is suffering badly from AMS, or Acute Mountain Sickness. Her face is beet red from sunburn and I guess she is also badly dehydrated. I tell her this, and she nods. Her boyfriend fetches a full bottle of water, which she drinks, pain etched in her face as she lies down afterwards on the bench seat. AMS is common. Go beyond 3,000 metres (or 10,000 feet) and three-fourths of all climbers will have at least mild symptoms. Who is and who isn't affected by altitude sickness is a crapshoot. By my own observations it's more common in athletic young men who climb too rapidly in an effort to prove their manliness. But there are no specific factors such as gender, age, or physical condition that will determine who gets AMS and who doesn't. Some people, like myself, are simply more susceptible and from what I've experienced, it doesn't seem to get better with over the years, or with the number of times one climbs to altitude.

Another trekker sits all by himself, not talking to anyone, staring vacantly at a blank piece of paper. I assume he has High Altitude Writer's Block. I can relate to his problem.

"We got shit-faced in Dingboche last night," a couple from Alaska tell us. "Hashish was so cheap and good, we couldn't say no."

There is another couple, a father and daughter. The daughter, probably early twenties, doesn't do anything for herself. Her father does it all, hangs her sweaty clothes to dry on the clothesline above the space heater, orders her food, and moves her chair so she is closer to the fire.

My headache becomes so bad I feel nauseous. I take painkillers, fetch my sleeping bag, and sit in the dining room beside the window and try to shake off the waves of nausea. Outside, I can see the sun setting on Ama Dablam, turning it yellow and then a brilliant gold. The others stay close to the space heater, ignoring the spectacular view outside. I order a small pot of hot lemon to get more liquid down me. The headache disappears, and so does the nausea, but the dry hacking cough starts. Every time I cough, the father of the daughter stares at me with eyes narrowed, as if I were coughing to deliberately annoy him. Or her.

Suffering from high altitude sickness can bring on irritability. So can a prissy pedantic father with an annoying accent and an equally annoying habit of not being able to stop giving advice to everyone within earshot. I study him closely and realise he was in the Panorama Lodge in Namche, with the South African group, the one led by the Sherpa with the sore feet. I had seen the South African, sitting in the corner of the Panorama lodge with a ruler and pen, making a ledger of some kind by writing columns of figures in intricate detail. I wagered then that he was an accountant. But where's the rest of the group now?

I half listen to his monologue. He talks about the magnificent home he owns in Sandton, an exclusive suburb of Johannesburg, and the short commuting distance to his work. And sure enough, he is an accountant. Because he's in his fifties and everyone else is younger, he feels it's his duty to dispense advice on any subject, to all of us. I wonder if his voice is really that tedious, or is it just me?

In the bad old days of apartheid, I spent a few years travelling around Southern Africa working for a Canadian-based non-governmental organization helping black South African refugees in Lesotho, Swaziland and Botswana. I was targeted by South African Intelligence as a Communist sympathiser, maybe even a member of the ANC, and shadowed by South African intelligence officers. South African secret forces abducted one of my black colleagues, machine-gunned another's home, and regularly broke into our offices to steal our files, despite our being in independent neighbouring countries. So many years later I am still easily irritated by the wrong kind of white South African. But The Accountant really does have an irksome voice, despite my subjectivity.

I stare out the window. Ama Dablam, bathed in the evening sunlight, is like a fantasy gold mountain rising out of the mist. Shadows slowly creep up its flanks until only the summit is bathed in the yellow light. Looking at all the mountains, it's as if someone drew a horizontal line with a ruler from summit to summit, with shadow below, golden light above. The tip of Ama Dablam turns a metallic blue-grey while the summit of Lhotse stays lit up, the yellow band on its flanks picking up the golden light. When the warm sunlight disappears off the mountains their aspect becomes cold and merciless. The four climbers on Ama Dablam must be down now.

The young Sherpa boy comes bouncing out of the kitchen whistling happily as he hands the South African daughter a bowl of soup.

"Do you run the lodge?" I ask, as he turns around to run back into the kitchen.

"No," he says, puffing out his chest proudly. "I am porter for him." He points at The Accountant.

"Look," The Accountant says to me, again not minding his own business. "He's like that in every lodge we stay. Always working. But rather that, than the opposite."

"What's your name?" I ask the boy.

"Chumba Sherpa," he replies. "I am pibteen."

He looks more like twelve than fifteen and although he is small, he's incredibly strong. I saw him carrying a large plastic container of water up from the stream by the bridge. It looked unbelievably heavy.

The Accountant prattles on, the sound of his own voice giving him some sense of comfort in this environment, so far from the reassuring confines of his magnificent home. He is an endless source of inanities.

"Is the *dal bhaat* deal per plate, or is it for as much as you can eat?" one of the Alaskans asks Chumba Sherpa.

"Look, I rather have a Big Mac," The Accountant interrupts. I've learned by now that he starts every other sentence with, "Look," or "Rather". If he does it one more time, I'm going to become an axe murderer. Make that an ice-pick murderer.

"Didn't I see you with a group of South Africans," I ask. "In Panorama Lodge in Namche?"

"That's right," he replies, suddenly defensive.

"What happened to your group?"

"Look, my daughter was sick with altitude, so they've gone ahead," he says. "Rather keep a porter and take our time."

He is obviously not happy about this decision. I gather by his reluctance to expand on the subject, given his eloquence on just about every other subject under the sun, that this is a sore and sensitive topic. I have the impression he is plotting his revenge on the tour operator with his careful summing of daily expenses. He has an irritating habit of snorting, almost as if he was snoring. When he doesn't talk, he snorts.

Unable to take much more of him, I step outside. Although the sun is no longer shining on Lhotse's flanks, the mountain seems to glow, as if it were a source of light radiating back rays absorbed during the day. It's a mountain far more dramatic in appearance than Everest. Its ridges are razor-sharp against a deepening cobalt blue sky. Despite the thick stone walls of the building, I can hear The Accountant's grating voice. He's commenting to the others, about viewing the sunset.

"Rather I bought a book with me on this trek," he says in that irksome accent. "Look, you watch the sunsets a couple of times, but not forever." Perhaps he is referring to my insistence on watching the setting sun.

When it gets too cold, I step back inside, reluctantly. The pressure light hanging over the space heater wanes and no one knows how do get it going again. With all the high-tech gadgets we can operate, we don't know how to prime a simple kerosene lantern? Kumar pumps the kerosene, priming it so the asbestos material glows brightly. Maybe that's what happens to the mountains just after sunset; someone pumps and primes them until they radiate light.

The conversation, of which I am not a part, turns to the cost of a Mars Bar.

This is a signal for me to turn in. But first, I get a second empty water bottle from the kitchen. Now I have two empty litre-bottles to fill up tonight. It's a symptom of altitude sickness that when the body dehydrates, no matter how much liquid you put in, more comes out.

I lie back and try to sleep. The sound of the hissing pressure lantern out in the dining room reminds me of growing up in Kenya, and the primitive cottage we had on the coast during the holidays. That was long before mass tourism. In the evenings we would all sit reading around the kerosene pressure lantern while moths and other insects fluttered around the bright light. There was one bedroom for the four of us, with the four beds pressed close together, side by side. Sometimes we'd have a pillow fight, bashing each other until someone cried, or our parents heard the ruckus. There was no television, not even electricity. We spent the days exploring the reefs, snorkelling above them or walking on them at low tide. Sometimes we would build human traps, pits carved into the sand, delicately excavated through a small hole, covered with sticks and leaves, and disguised with a thin layer of sand. We gleefully hid in the rocks and waited for unsuspecting fishermen to come walking along the shore. But the only humans we ever trapped were ourselves.

Years later, posted to Tanzania by the United Nations Development Programme, I quickly fell in love with the country. Its borders were closed to Kenya at the time, and tourism was almost dead after years of socialism. But that made living in this East African country all the more exclusive. When I quit the bureaucratic UN to run the private safari business in Tanzania, I had two boats, four Landrovers, a Cessna 182 and some thirty African staff to help me run the camp. I begged Kevin for a year to come and visit but it was always difficult for him to take time off. Finally he came out to pay a visit. We were both single and carefree. It would be our last adventure together.

13

Duglha-Lobuche Communal Beds

I take my time in the morning so that the others in the lodge will move ahead. I intend to climb slowly and if I let them go first, by "them" I mean The Accountant, I should be able to walk in the gap between this wave and the first wave of trekkers climbing up from Pheriche and Dingboche. Half way up the hill I come across Chumba Sherpa singing happily. He's carrying both The Accountant's huge expedition duffel bags and his daughter's. The bags must weigh thirty-kilos each. Pemba seems to have unlimited energy, but the weight of his burden has slowed him down. His face drips with perspiration, but he still finds the energy to sing. He laughs and smiles at me when I tease him about going so slowly.

A trickle of trekkers descends. The purge of hikers I had seen escaping the mountains earlier was obviously not the full complement of trekkers returning from Everest Base Camp. The walk to Lobuche is tucked beside the lateral moraine of the Khumbu Glacier. On the left, on the other side of a small valley and stream, is the path contouring the flanks of a steep hill up the valley to Dzonglha and the Cho La pass into the Gokyo Valley. I bump into three of the British Army group coming down. Two of them have altitude problems and are being escorted back down to Pheriche to see the doctors there.

Lobuche is nothing more than a couple of scruffy lodges on a flat piece of yak pasture at the foot of the Lobuche Peak and the Lobuche Glacier. The only accommodation is in dormitories on shared platform bunks. I move in to the largest of the lodges, put my pack on a foam mattress and scatter a few clothes to secure my slice of bed for the night. There's a desolate feel about the place and it's obvious that the supply route up here is sketchy at best. No wonder Mingma Sherpa, at Deboche, wanted to open a good lodge here. He'd have no competition and he could charge what he wanted.

A trekker from a camping group walks into the rustic shelter and asks to use the phone. He looks ill. Surprisingly, there is indeed a telephone sitting conspicuously on a plank of wood. The Sherpa manager dials the number given him and within seconds the sick-looking trekker is talking to his family somewhere in the States. "Just wanted to let you know I'm fine," he says, lying. He looks terrible and is obviously suffering from altitude sickness. His hair is matted, he's unshaven, and his eyes have sunk into his skull. From the conversation, it's clear he misses his family. "Wish you were here," he says. "I'll be back soon." He puts down the telephone and is instantly cut off from his family by several walking days and a couple of long flights halfway around the world. He pays for the call and is escorted out by his solicitous Sherpa guide.

Two trekkers arrive wearing plastic climbing boots, the kind of heavy boots crampons can be attached to. They carry their own packs, have ice picks attached on the outside of their rucksacks, and carry telescoping walking sticks. They have just come over the Cho La pass from Gokyo.

"What was it like?" I ask, eager to know whether I should take this shortcut to Gokyo Lakes rather than walk down the valley and around.

"Icy," one of them replies. "We got lost in the snow near the top for over two hours and couldn't find our way. You need to have an ice pick at least, to cross over now, and it would be better with crampons, especially if you are coming from this side because it is slipperier on the other side. To go down where it is slippery is more difficult than going up."

Good point. I still might have taken the chance if I weren't so unconfident of my back. The way it is, I'm just too vulnerable, should I fall and twist it the wrong way.

A blonde man suffering an altitude headache sits next to me. We talk for a few minutes. A doctor working for Lufthansa, his job is to medically examine the airline's pilots. I ask him how he qualified for that position.

"I was interested in the effects of flying on the human body," he says. "The biggest problem for commercial pilots is the constant adjustment to different time zones."

He's also a pilot, which is a necessary condition for his job with Lufthansa. He shares a private plane with three other pilots and, in addition, he's a glider pilot instructor. In his spare time, he travels or run marathons. I guess he is about forty years old. When I ask if he's married, he tells me no. It's hardly surprising. With a schedule like he has, he'd never have time to fit in a woman.

"Because I suffer bad altitude sickness from a very low altitude," he goes on to tell me, "I have to go more slowly than others." He looks at his watch. "So I try to climb high each day and sleep low. Now I will walk to Gorak Shep and come back."

He doesn't have much time, although if he's used to doing marathons, he's probably in good shape. At these altitudes, I cannot climb vertically more than three hundred metres a day. But I've only walked a couple of hours today so I too, continue towards Gorak Shep, telling Kumar that I'll be back in a couple of hours. The ground is rough, and the path dodges in and out of boulders brought down from the mountains by the glacier when it was larger and wider. At a sign posted *Hotel 8,000* I divert into a portal in the rocks. Walking along the narrow cleft I soon come across a structure in the shape of a pyramid, the front all glass windowpanes. Next to it, I recognise the bright yellow mess tents of The Patriarch's group.

I had read about "The Pyramid." In 1990, the Royal Nepal Academy of Science and Technology agreed to let the Italian National Research Centre install a scientific laboratory here, as a high-altitude research centre. Built on a slope and shaped like a pyramid, "The Pyramid" quickly became its nickname. The laboratory is built here because this is one of the highest inhabited places in the world. I suspect the portal in the rocks not only protects the structure from wandering trekkers by keeping it out of sight and out of mind, but also protects it from winds, too.

Through the glass windowpanes on the ground floor, I see a kitchen with tiled floors, and a basic dining room. Upstairs, there are private rooms with beds covered in duvets.

"Is possible to stay here?" I ask.

"For twenty-five dollars," one of The Patriarch's guides tells me.

Anywhere else in the world, twenty-five dollars to sleep in a comfortable lodge would not seem excessive. Here, where most lodges cost a dollar to a dollar and a half, those rates seem exorbitant. Although the Americans are staying here, they are nowhere to be found, probably on their way to Gorak Shep themselves.

I return the way I came, through the protective portal, and then up along the bouldered pathway until I can see the black hill that is Kala Pattar. From this vantage point the climb up Kala Pattar looks insignificants, a stroll up a molehill.

From the small spur of the path overlooking the intersection of the Changri Glacier and the Khumbu Glacier, I watch clouds stream off the summit of Lhotse and the nipple summit of Everest seen behind Nuptse. Apart from the occasional crash of an avalanche, and the distant tinkling of yak bells, it is perfectly silent.

Despite drinking copious amounts of water, I am still fighting an altitude headache. When I return to Lobuche I take my first 125 grams of Diamox. Acetazolamide, sold under the trade name Diamox, is a carbonic anhydrase inhibitor. Knowing I suffer from altitude sickness I take the pill as a last resort to force my kidneys to excrete bicarbonate, the conjugate base of carbonic acid. By increasing the amount of bicarbonate excreted in the urine, the blood becomes more acidic and acidifying the blood stimulates ventilation, which is beneficial during acclimatization. After taking the pill I sit outside with several Nepalese men to bask in the last rays of warm sunlight. Kumar has already informed me that he is staying at a rustic stone shelter away from the four lodges. The prices he would be charged for food at my lodge makes it too expensive for him.

In no time, the sun dips below the ridge of mountains. From a sunny courtyard, we are suddenly sitting in a cold and rather bleak environment. A Grumpy Couple who haven't stopped complaining about one thing or another since I've been here, exit the lodge. The food is awful, the lodges are dirty, the porters are lazy, and the Sherpas are overcharging. On and on, they carp. I overhear their conversation with their porter, a small Sherpa boy who couldn't be more than fifteen.

"We go to Dzonglha now," The Grumpy Man says. "Tomorrow we go over Cho La to Gokyo."

The porter, who doesn't speak much English, shakes his head, refusing. Another Sherpa translates for him.

"He says he does not want to go because he has never been over the pass before, and he has heard that it is slippery with ice now."

From what I was just told about the pass and the icy conditions up there, it sounds like a wise decision the young Sherpa has made. But the Grumpy Couple is not pleased with this news.

"When we hired him in Dingboche he said he would come over the pass with us," The Grumpy Man declares.

"But he is scared," says the impromptu translator. "He has heard from porters and guides who have come the other way that it is slippery now, and dangerous. He does not have the experience to be your guide. You are employing him only as your porter."

"If he doesn't come, then we do not pay him," Grumpy says.

The Sherpa boy is unmoved by the threat. He shakes his head again. The translator looks back at Grumpy Man.

"He says he will not cross the Cho La."

Grumpy Man becomes visibly angry and impatient. He swears loudly in his own language. He's tall and athletic, towering over the boy.

"He has only carried our packs from Gorak Shep today," Grumpy snarls. "If he doesn't come, we pay him nothing. He can go back to Dingboche."

The boy has been paid on a daily basis, getting his salary at the end of each day. Still, he says nothing, nor does his translator. None of the other Nepalese sitting in the clump, watching, says anything. They all avoid looking at the Grumpy Couple. Grumpy Man gives vent to his frustrations by swearing loudly but unintelligibly at his recalcitrant porter as the irate couple re-pack their packs.

The owner of the lodge comes out. He's an older and far more experienced Sherpa. I'm sure he has probably seen and heard everything from Westerners. The Sherpa who has been translating recounts what's happened. The lodge owner stares angrily at the Grumpy Couple, but he too says nothing.

It takes the pair a few precious minutes to sort through their belongings and rearrange the contents. They had given their young Sherpa the larger pack filled with the heaviest items and are now redistributing the weight. By the time they're ready to go, it's already four in the afternoon. It takes two to four hours to walk to Dzonglha, which means they will be arriving after dark. They leave, without paying the boy for carrying their packs down from Gorak Shep. When they disappear from sight the boy, who now has no clients and no source of income, self-consciously leaves the group of Nepalese and begins his return to Dingboche.

Embarrassed that he should be so ill treated by fellow Westerners, I lope after him and discretely hand him three one hundred rupee notes. He accepts the money with gratitude, but his eyes reflect his humiliation and loss of face.

When I return to the dormitory, I take warm clothes from my pack. The room has several sticks of burning incense to hide the smell of dirty socks and other odorous items from the unwashed trekkers and their staff. Although the lodge had been empty when I arrived this morning, it is now full. In the one dormitory, all the bunk beds are taken and mattresses have been placed on the floor. There is almost no room on the floor to access the platform bed.

Reluctant to turn in for the day, I wander around Lobuche. As I walk by one of the other lodges I bump into Christina.

"I was looking for you," she tells me. "One of the soldiers said he'd seen you. Where are you staying?"

"There." I point to my lodge. "What have you been up to today?"

"Climbed Kala Pattar."

"Already?" I ask. Many of the trekkers who climb Kala Pattar do so from here rather than sleep at a higher altitude at Gorak Shep, the original site for the Everest base camps.

"We set off before dawn this morning and returned this afternoon," Christina says. "Two of the soldiers got badly dehydrated because their plastic water containers had frozen solid during the night. For the first two hours they had nothing to drink. Kala Pattar was a zoo. There was a French group there and they refused to move from the summit. There's only a few big rocks up there, so if you want your photo taken at the top, you have to wait your turn. But they wouldn't get off. Just opened their picnic lunches and sat there eating. So the soldiers pulled down their pants and bent over butt naked and mooned them until they moved."

We sit outside my lodge on Styrofoam sheets, watching the fading light on the mountains, especially Lhotse. Although I had met Christina only briefly a couple of times three years earlier while travelling around New Zealand, we had connected then, and like many travellers, had talked from the heart. We had remained in sporadic touch after that but lost contact recently. It's good to see her again.

As it gets colder and darker I ask, "Want a hot lemon?"

We go inside my lodge to the dining room, which is crowded with a Japanese family of five, and another Australian group.

"How much does it costs to sleep here?" I overhear an Aussie ask the Sherpa owner. The owner calculates the rupees into Australian dollars.

"And how much is it to rent a blanket for the night?"

The owner computes the exchange and holds up the calculator

"And how much for two blankets?" the Aussie asks.

A Nepalese porter comes out of the kitchen and shoves plastic water bottles and wrappings into the space heater to burn, producing toxic fumes. Another group of Nepalese porters leaf through a woman's magazine. They giggle and laugh self-consciously as they point at the ads with semi-naked women. Their giggles are mixed with bouts of coughing.

Many of the trekkers are here for a second night, having walked up to Gorak Shep early in the morning, climbed up to the summit of Kala Pattar, and then back down to Lobuche. They sit around the tables, looking shattered. Many of them wear cheap Made-in-China imitation North Face equipment. One man is slumped immobile over the dining table. A Sherpa guide sits next to him, his arm thrown comfortingly over his client's back.

I go outside again to relieve myself in the bitter cold. Peeing against the stone walls of the lodge, I can see the Sherpa owner through a window in his private room. He's lying in bed, with a bedside table covered in lotions, candles, and photographs. He does not notice me watching him, warm inside his single bed as he rubs lotion all over his face and hands, and then blows out the candle to sleep.

The kitchen is chaos as orders for food are prepared. A large, healthy-looking Sherpa woman, the owner's wife, busily oversees operations. I mention to her how comfortable her husband looked, swaddled in bed.

"You too like a private room and bed?" she asks, laughing. "No problem. I tell him get out and you go in. Forty dollars per night."

For forty dollars a night, she'll throw her husband out of bed.

"That price includes you?" I ask, teasing.

"Up to you," she says, still laughing.

A trekker pokes his head into the kitchen.

"Is there somewhere I can wash?" he asks.

"No,' the Sherpa woman tells him.

"Dumb question I guess," the trekker admits.

Christina squeezes in next to me at the dinner table. By eight in the evening, everyone has headed for bed. I walk Christina back to her nearby lodge and then return to mine. With all the common bunks, and every mattress on the floor occupied, I crawl into my sleeping bag. Next to me on one side is a Sherpa guide for the Japanese family. On my other side is an older Australian, the man who was slumped over the table. He looks as if he might not make it through the night

"Are you a snorer?" I ask him.

"Snore?" he replies. "I'm a non-sleeper at the moment and if I do manage to go to sleep, I'll be lucky if I wake up."

I squeeze in my wax earplugs, and am about to fall asleep when I remember the Lufthansa doctor. His sleeping bag was on the other side of the Australian. He was heading up to Gorak Shep and should already be back here for the night. I sit up, wondering what I should do. I consider asking the British Army to go and rescue him. I get out of my sleeping bag, step over the slumbering bodies on the floor, and into the dining room. Who do I alert? I am still considering the options when the door to the lodge suddenly opens and in walks the German doctor. By the light of his flashlight I can see the exhaustion on his face.

"What happened?" I ask. "I was about to raise the alarm."

"I went further than I thought," he smiles proudly. "To Kala Pattar."

"You went from here to the top of Kala Pattar and back again to Lobuche in one afternoon and evening?" I'm incredulous. "That must have been difficult with the ice."

"I didn't know how long the batteries in my torch would last," he says, "so I used it as little as possible. I saw the sunset on Kala Pattar and then came down to Gorak Shep but the path here is hard to follow sometimes because of the snow and the boulders. It was almost impossible at night." He laughs, still high on the adrenaline rush and the endorphins. "Would you take a photo of me?" He pulls out a small camera and I take a photo of a very exhausted German doctor. Jamie's book estimates the distance to be a minimum of a four-hour to a maximum of seven-hour walk for the one-way trip, but the German has done the return trip in six hours, two hours of it in the dark, on a difficult trail.

We climb over the bodies on the floor and crawl onto the platform bunk. As soon as I lie down, my stomach turns and I feel nauseous. Every little sign of sickness can be ascribed to altitude sickness: headaches, nausea, fatigue, loss of appetite, coughing. But this churning in my stomach has nothing to do with the altitude. I try to ignore it but I can't. I extricate myself from my sleeping bag, step over the wall-to-wall porters, guides and trekkers asleep on the floor, and step outside under a three-quarters moon that shines brightly over Everest and Lhotse.

The toilet is locked, presumably to stop the army of passing trekkers from using the facilities. For those of us staying here, we have to ask for the key. But whom do I get the key from at this time of night? Everyone inside is asleep. I don't have time to debate the question and squat hurriedly over the ledge and void myself.

Everyone I spoke to coming down the trail had told me they had been sick at Lobuche. I am no exception to the rule. Feeling guilty for the mess I have created, I enter the lodge and crawl back into my sleeping bag. The stomach cramps have stopped, but now I feel tingling in the soles of my feet and in my fingers from the Diamox pills I have been taking. At least I don't have the persistent headache anymore. I cough and for the first time since Lukla, it doesn't feel as if my brain is rattling around loosely inside my skull.

⚜

14

Lobuche-Gorak Shep
Everest Base Camp

In the morning I sit next to the Australian. His face is as grey as his hair. He is slumped over and at first I wonder if he's even alive.

"Are you okay?" I ask to make sure.

He blinks his eyes several times before he turns to look at me. "I woke up."

"That's a start," I say. I try to pour my cough syrup, but it's almost frozen solid.

Everyone huddles miserably around their cups of tea, except the three Japanese children who play happily with a dog that clearly hasn't had this kind of attention before. The Japanese children are having the time of their lives. The mother tries to make herself presentable with the help of a tiny mirror, and makeup, and lipstick. Her husband, longhaired and long-bearded, is more casual about his appearance as he warms his hands by the space heater.

The lodge owner I'd observed going to bed early last night doesn't participate in any of the lodge activities except for collecting money from trekkers before they leave. A lowly porter who had worked his way up to the position of trekking *sirdar*, his role now is to count the money pouring into the coffers of the lodge he leases. Both his large wife and the cook double-check each bill. I doubt they would overlook a consumed cup of milk tea. The owner handles a wad of money as thick as a New York phone book. A few seasons doing this and the family would be set up for life in Nepal. Working a lifetime at this, and they'd be able to retire reasonably in Miami.

My stomach still isn't better. I ask for the key to the outdoor drop toilet. When I see the mess of excrement on the wooden floorboards, I'm thankful I didn't come in here during the night with my bare feet in flip-flops.

Kumar arrives and we set off together, the wind blowing hard in our faces. We seem to be the only ones heading up. The trekkers we meet coming downhill move fast, eager to get to lower altitudes as quickly as possible. They've all done their big climb, reached Everest Base Camp, or Gorak Shep, and some have climbed Kala Pattar, their own minor version of the legendary Everest summit. Now they are desperate to get lower, to better food and lodging. "Trek fatigue" the Australian had termed the quiet desperation he had felt.

The path alongside the Khumbu Glacier is slippery. It is often difficult to tell whether one is stepping on the surface of a boulder, dirt-covered ice, or snow. I skid onto my ass a couple of times and each time I fall, I feel a muscle spasm in my back. It's a frightening insight into how treacherous the Cho La might be. The small daypack I carry is loaded with solid camera equipment and falling on it could do my fragile back an injury. Although I am confident the vertebra has knitted together, the torn ligaments and muscles are still tender. The falls confirm my decision that it would be better for me to return to Pangboche and then walk all the way up the Gokyo Valley. It'll take me longer, but I won't risk injury. But now, after crossing the massive Khangri Glacier and climbing over its lateral moraine ridgeline, Gorak Shep is directly below to the north, while to the south, for the first time, is an extended view of the lower portion of the Khumbu Glacier

It is an anticlimax having walked all this way up here to see that Gorak Shep is nothing more than two lodges beside a frozen pond covered in snow. Tibetan snow cocks waddle around like oversized pigeons. They are pretty birds, more the size of a duck than a pigeon, with distinctive black and white stripes and a brown-grey body supported by orange legs. I take out my camera and cautiously snap several photos from a distance until I realise that they are perfectly tame. They pluck unsuccessfully at bits of rubbish sticking out from a bamboo basket containing litter. The yellow-billed choughs, however, are more adept at flying onto the edge of the basket and pulling out plastic wrappers, which they fling aside with the professionalism of discerning pickpockets. It's sad seeing these masters of aerial acrobatics reduced to the level of scavengers of human refuse.

A longhaired and bearded Westerner wearing wind-proof pants and a turtleneck shirt sits in a plastic chair outside a lodge, protected from the wind. Inside I am told there are so few trekkers now that I can have a single room to myself. Basic, with a rough stone floor and insulated with sheets of Styrofoam stapled to the walls, I can sleep on my own bed without having neighbours on either side rolling over me during the night. Chumba Sherpa is there, already laughing and joking and helping out in the kitchen. If I didn't know he was The Accountant's porter, I would think he was one of the staff at the lodge.

I pull up a chair and sit near the American who is dressed as if to go skiing. "I've been here two weeks," he tells me, "studying the alpine meadow there." He points at the slope of Kala Pattar. The black "hill" doesn't look quite so small from this perspective. In fact, it looms four hundred plus metres above us. "This kind of alpine meadow," the American continues, "so high up and with such a wide variety of flora on it is rare, but trekkers are ruining it. They should stay on the one path." He points at the slope. "Look how there are several paths leading up. Whenever it rains or snows and gets muddy, trekkers walk adjacent to the established path to avoid the slippery mud. If that keeps happening, they'll destroy the alpine meadow entirely."

"Have you spoken to the park officials about this?"

He laughs cynically. "I've even gone to Park Headquarters in Kathmandu. The officials sit on their asses all day smoking, drinking tea and reading the newspapers. I had an appointment with the Park Warden and he couldn't answer my simplest questions. They are useless. You don't see anything that the Government has done for the Park, despite all the money they get from the ten dollars entrance fee they collect from trekkers. It must amount to a quarter of a million dollars a year and that's not even including the fees they collect from the climbers who climb the summits. I've been in Nepal on a scholarship programme and it's the same in all the Government departments. The corruption here and the inefficiency make me sick. I'm leaving day after tomorrow and can hardly wait to get out of here." His mirror sunglasses conceal his eyes. "You hear so much about the hospitality of the Sherpas," he continues, "but I haven't seen any of that. They're all too busy making money and trying to get to America."

He has been sleeping these weeks in a tent some ten metres from the lodge. He points out where the cairn erected to Rob Hall is, and where Everest Base Camp is. The thought of getting to the present-day Base Camp doesn't have much appeal; there is no one there, no tents, nothing. And besides, the view of Everest is far better from the top of Kala Pattar.

Chumba Sherpa exits the lodge to fetch water with a huge empty plastic container from the other side of the frozen lake. I follow him and then cross the snow-covered ice to a small ridgeline that leads to a spur and several cairns. Unprotected from the wind, the cold breeze bites into the flesh. There is no sign of life, and no one else around. Somewhere amidst all that snow and ice, is the modern Everest Base Camp. It's absolutely quiet as I reach the first of several cairns connected to another with a line of prayer flags. The second more substantial cairn with a better view is erected to the memory of Rob Hall, the New Zealander climber best known for being head guide of the ill-fated 1996 Mount Everest expedition. At the time of his death, Hall held the record for ascending Everest more times than any other non-Sherpa. Hall spoke to his wife, Jan Arnold, by phone from the mountain before he perished. Two months after his death, Jan gave birth to their first child. Annabel had gone to medical school with Jan in Dunedin, New Zealand.

Annabel has been a medical doctor for two Everest marathons. It's impossible to imagine runners walking all the way up here from Lukla or Jiri and then running a marathon from here to Namche, up to Thame and back to Namche again. Annabel has shown me videos taken during these races. It boggles my mind that anyone would attempt it. It's even more mind boggling that anyone would attempt to climb Everest.

It has been such a struggle getting to Gorak Shep it's beyond the realm of possibility for me to imagine climbing an additional three thousand metres from here to get to the summit of Everest.

I sit on a rock ledge of one of the cairns erected to another dead mountain climber and scan the scenery around the spur. It's impressive, no doubt, but it doesn't instil in me a feeling that I would want to cremate my envelope here.

At the lodge, the owner estimates the climb to the top of Kala Pattar at one to two hours. I leave Gorak Shep at 3 pm, hoping it will take me one and a half hours to climb to the summit. My rationale in heading up so late is that no one else will be there, leaving me to watch the sunset on my own.

The beginning of the walk is steep, and then it flattens out until it becomes steep again. It's difficult to determine where the path is; there is a metre of snow on the ground and in the winter light it's not easy to see the indentations where the path has been trodden down. When the sun disappears behind the mountains the warm friendly light around me dissipates. It's frightening, and yet I walk higher even as my instincts tell me to go down. Not for the first time, I can imagine what it must be like to be a real high-altitude climber. A bit like diving in the ocean; down ten metres doesn't make a lot of difference. But dive beyond thirty metres and the danger level rises dramatically.

As the sun sinks further the tidemark of shadow rises up the flanks of Lhotse and Everest. It's a race against time now and it's taking me longer to climb than I thought it would. I try to increase my pace but it feels as if my heart will burst, literally. I don't have a headache, thanks to the Diamox I took just before I started the climb, but the exertion in ascending so fast makes me fight for air, as if I'm drowning.

I question whether I am doing the right thing, climbing alone ever higher as the sun's rays disappear from the surrounding mountains. The desolation and the extreme conditions of these high Himalayas become very real. But I keep hiking, drawn by the top of Kala Pattar, which is still in sunlight. I force myself to keep moving, to reach the top while there is still sunlight. But all I really want to do is stop and rest. My lungs feel seared and my head throbs from the fast, non-stop effort. I know that if I rest I'll reach the summit of Kala Pattar after the sun has gone and the feeling will be even more desolate. I press on.

The walk is no longer a stroll and I have to scramble amongst rocks and boulders. Looking up ahead, I see the American researcher. His presence is both a welcome and unwelcome sight. I wanted to be alone on the top of Kala Pattar. On the other hand, there's comfort in numbers. Lungs bursting, I reach the top, gasping for breath. The sun is still just above the summit of mountains to the west.

"You made it," he says to me.

"Just," I wheeze, and then cough uncontrollably.

We remain silent, watching the sun set on Everest and the lesser but more spectacular summits surrounding us. Standing on the boulder looking vertically down the precipice carved away long ago by a massive glacier, gives me vertigo. Immediately below, in the direction of Everest, is a lake. Further to the right is the modern day Everest Base Camp, indistinguishable from the rest of the valley because there are no climbing expeditions there now.

Stretching down the valley is the Khumbu Glacier. The view is without a doubt, extraordinary. If you can't climb Everest, this is definitely the next best thing. I had become blasé about the walk up to Gorak Shep. I haven't wanted to admit it to anyone, least of all myself, but the walk up to Everest Base Camp has been disappointing. But on the summit of this molehill called Kala Pattar, the views of the mountains around are nothing short of incredible; I've never been in such awe at the sight of so many mountains so high above. The scale of things is totally out of proportion to anything else I've ever experienced. Nothing has prepared me for this stupendous view, not even being in the middle of the Annapurna Sanctuary at Annapurna Base Camp compares to this.

The walk up here has been so dominated by tourism that at times there seemed little left of the original Sherpa culture, architecture and way of life. That is a misleading perspective born of walking here in the trekking season, along the trekking corridors. The landscape has been spectacular, although it is desolate and the immediate views often limited by terminal and lateral moraines. But the view from Kala Pattar is fabulous beyond description, and yet this is only a glimpse of what it must be like for those on the top of any of the surrounding peaks. Here, on the top of Kala Pattar at only 5,600 metres, I can look down at the long tongue of the Khumbu Glacier in its entirety. The solitude, the disappearing light, the cold, and the icy fingers of fear gripping my shoulders as darkness sets in exaggerate this insight into what it must be like at the top of Everest.

I wait until the last bit of direct light on the top of Everest has disappeared. Venus pokes over its summit. It is absolutely silent. I turn around to look for my companion. He's sitting quietly, contemplative.

"I'm heading down," I tell him. The light is fading fast and, stupidly, I don't have a flashlight. It's almost half past five.

"I'm staying for a while," the American says. "It's my last night here and I want to savour the experience."

"See you at the bottom then." It doesn't even occur to me that I might want to burn the envelope up here.

I know we should stay together but I am anxious to get down. And I want to be respectful of his wishes to be alone. I scramble down the boulders. It's a race against time to get down to the bottom before it is completely dark. At first, the ambient light is sufficient to see the path. But the undefined snow trail in the diminishing luminosity makes it difficult to see, and there are several routes leading down. I step on the solid ice in the centre of the trodden pathway but occasionally step to the side and sink up to my knee in snow. I maintain my momentum, keen to get down as quickly as possible. The temperature is already numbingly cold and I don't want to spend the night up here.

To my left and below, I see the light of the American's torch. Somehow he has passed me by. I am probably too far to the right. I stagger down the hill until I am almost on the edge of the steep ridge immediately overlooking Gorak Shep. I stumble consistently now, both from fatigue and the darkness. I can see the light of the lodge, but there is a black chasm between me and it. My pace on this steep section is reduced to that of a snail. I have to feel ahead with my boots before I can take a single step. The sky is black with the sharp pinpricks of stars, and it will probably be an hour or so before the moon comes up. I look at my watch. Seven o'clock. I can't remember what time the moon rises over the summits of the mountains. The mountains are high enough it could be some hours. I know I'll be able to see my way in the moonlight but for now I can't see a thing and it'll be cold waiting. I have completely lost the path on this precipitous slope. The small ledges I step on seem to be a labyrinth of yak paths. I feel with boot and walking stick, trying to make my way down. I can't conceive of doing this from the summit of Everest.

From below, where the lodge should be, I see a flashlight moving across what must be the frozen lake. Hopefully someone has come out to find me. I whistle loudly and someone whistles back. I wait patiently and whistle occasionally so that whoever it is can make his way up to me. It only takes him fifteen minutes. It's Kumar. I feel like hugging him.

"Thanks Kumar," I say, as I follow him down the path.

When we enter the lodge all eyes turn to us. The Accountant and his daughter, the Alaskan couple, and three other men look up and stare at me. For the first time, I've changed sides. I've graduated. I am no longer Going Up, I'm Going Down. I have status. I'm somebody with valuable first-hand information that everyone else Going Up wants. I saunter through the dining area and into my room where I change out of perspiration-soaked clothes into a dry set. The room itself is numbingly cold. Steam rises off my clothes. I unpack my bag, lay all the necessities for the night around the head of the bed and then go back to the dining room.

I'm too worn out to have an appetite but I feel curiously satiated too.

The Accountant is conspicuously quiet tonight.

"Did you just come down from Kala Pattar?" Someone asks me.

"Yes," I reply, neglecting to add that I had to be rescued by my porter.

"What was it like?" someone else asks.

I echo what I had been told repeatedly by Those Going Down when I asked the same question.

"It's fabulous," I answer. "For those of us who don't have a head for heights, lots of money, or a mountaineering background, it's amazing. The next best thing to climbing Everest." Maybe I can understand why climbers climb Everest after all. Their feelings of accomplishment must be a thousand times what I'm feeling right now.

I can feel it. Everyone else in the room can feel it, too.
Magic.

15

Gorak Shep-Pangboche

I sleep well, both from exhaustion and the fact that, at long last, I don't have a headache. Lying in my ultra-warm sleeping bag, trying to muster the discipline to get up, I feel the tingling in my fingers and soles of my feet from the Diamox. The urine in the half-filled water bottle is frozen opaque rather than being clear, a bad sign that I am dehydrated again. It's so cold the windows have a thick layer of frozen condensation obscuring the view and my pen won't write when I try to make an entry in my diary. I get up for breakfast.

Chumba Sherpa sings happily as he shoves frozen yak dung into the space heater. He has this curious habit of constantly flicking his wrist clear of his sleeve to check the time. The metal strap on the watch is too big for him and the watch hangs limply off his wrist. I assume the watch is a relatively new acquisition and his constant referral to it is not so much Chumba's pressing need to know the time as a reassuring look at something he is proud of owning. We sit huddled around the space heater for warmth as the sun begins to warm the dining room.

"Did you climb on any expeditions?" I ask the owner of the lodge who is from Khunde. He used to work as a cook at Everest Base Camp. He shakes his head.

"No, I don't want to climb," he says. "It is too dangerous." He looks admiringly at his wife holding a baby, its naked bottom exposed, despite the cold. The baby is spotlessly clean and cute as can be. When he urinates over the mother she just laughs and wipes up the liquid after handing the baby over to the father.

The Accountant limps into the room, conspicuously quiet.

"What happened?" I ask, looking at his feet.

"Twisted my ankle walking to Everest Base Camp," he replies with self-importance. "Look, you must visit the place if you are interested in climbing. I've read books on climbing Everest, so for me it was worth it."

"Is there anything to see?" I ask.

"No." He snorts like a horse, but strangely enough, it doesn't irritate me at all and I realise its because I don't have that persistent headache. I have finally acclimatised after two weeks walking and 250 milligrams of Diamox. It feels wonderful not having a throbbing head and my irritability on the way up here has dissipated. I even feel sorry for The Accountant, with his twisted ankle and his shifty little eyes.

"Are you going up Kala Pattar?" I ask, now that I am a veteran.

"Rather go to Everest Base Camp," he replies with another snort.

"But you can't even get a view of Everest from there," I counter.

"No," he agrees.

"Beautiful outlook of Everest from the top of Kala Pattar," I tell him. "Superb views of everything from up there. Too bad you twisted your ankle."

His daughter comes into the dining room looking decidedly petulant.

"What's the matter?" her father asks.

"The toilets out the back, they're disgusting," she says, her contorted face a mask of revulsion.

Chumba continues serving everyone breakfasts. Kumar eats his *dal bhaat* and I ask to pay my bill. Like a horse heading back to the stables, Kumar is packed and ready to go. After these days hiking together he has a tacit understanding of what I'm likely to do each day and he anticipates our movements eagerly. I'm beginning to trust him implicitly. He's almost running as we descend from Kala Pattar. Trekkers heading up ask me how Kala Pattar was.

"Great," I say. "You can't believe the view until you are on the top. I was sceptical right up to the last twenty minutes." I'm relishing my role as the newly initiated. I'd be unbearable if I actually climbed Everest. On the other hand, I probably wouldn't have the need to be unbearable if I'd climbed Everest.

Heading south into the sun now is like being baked in a solar oven. A couple of hours later, by the time I get to Lobuche, I feel as if I'm strolling through a familiar neighbourhood park. Outside the lodge I had stayed in are two rows of bright orange tents, lined up with military precision, not a millimetre out of line. White-haired tourists sit in folding canvas chairs drinking tea and reading, their porters wearing matching overalls. The guides wear their own brand of matching outfit: Oakley mirrored sunglasses, authentic North Face jackets, and plastic climbing boots.

I stop to look at the tops of the mountains. Just as it is fascinating to think that a few select men have made it to the moon and back, so too is it fascinating to think that a few brave men and women have made it to the top of Everest. But I can't help feeling that the traffic jams of climbers, their competitiveness, the callousness with which climbers leave others to die, or walk by their frozen bodies, is a sad reflection of their egotism.

Further down I have to step aside for a line of porters carrying pots and pans, iron dining tables, folding chairs, kerosene stoves, containers, stoves and even a toilet seat. Reading the books, or watching films on the climbing expeditions, I was struck by the lack of credit given to the Sherpas who set up the camps, carried the supplies, and cooked the food. Even the Everest Imax film discretely hid the fact that an army of Sherpas had to have carried all that heavy camera equipment up to the top of Everest. You certainly don't see any of that activity in the film. The books and films are so Western-centric. Watching these porters nonchalantly carry loads of as much as one hundred kilos confirms the assertion that any Sherpa could make it to the top of Everest. Just give them the equipment, warm clothes, boots, and crampons, have fixed ropes already set up for them, give them oxygen, provide them with tents, sleeping bags, and cups of tea, soup and plates of hot food whenever they required it, and I am quite sure every able-bodied Sherpa could make it to the top of Everest if they wanted to.

Several breathless trekkers bundled in a protective group ask me how far it is to Lobuche. Now that I am acclimatised and descending it is strange to see how out of breath they are as they ascend. At the ridge overlooking Duglha, the trekkers coming up the steep hill seem to be moving in slow motion. Those passing me by on the way up want to talk because it gives them an excuse to catch their breath. Distances shrink now that I'm acclimatized to .the high altitude and have the force of gravity helping me descend.

Before midday, I reach Duglha, under an immaculate blue sky. Although my headache has gone, my stomach muscles are tender from a persistent cough. I try to breathe through my nose so the air entering my throat might gain some moisture. At the large lodge in Pheriche I stop to have lunch. I join Chumba Sherpa in the kitchen and order yak curry, the same as the porters. Kumar eats with me and although he has to pay the same amount as I do for a meal, he manages to tuck into three full helpings for the same price.

"Is this really yak meat or buffalo meat?" I ask the cook, the beautiful Sherpa girl called Tzangpo. Although there are no buffalo at these altitudes, I suspect that it isn't really yak meat, just as some of the "yak bone" jewellery isn't really yak bone, and the "yak" wool sweaters aren't really yak wool, and "yak" or "*nak*" cheese isn't really *nak* cheese. Westerners have this insatiable appetite for anything made from yaks.

"Buffalo meat from Namche," she replies. The buffalo meat bought in Namche comes from lower down the valley because there are no buffalo in Namche either.

Helicopter blades thump the air and a few minutes later a helicopter hovers overhead and lands outside the Himalayan Rescue Association clinic.

"An evacuation?" I ask Tzangpo.

"A Japanese woman with altitude sickness," she replies without emotion.

While Tzangpo and her mother work hard in the kitchen preparing meals, a young Sherpa man with long hair lies sprawled on a bed in the kitchen, reading magazines by the light of an adjacent window. I don't recognise him as the brother although from his body language, I assume he must be a son. When I ask Tzangpo how much the "yak" curry costs, she asks the young man. He doesn't bother to look up from his magazine as he replies in his own dialect.

"One hundred and fifty rupees," she tells me.

The Accountant sticks his head into the kitchen to ask for a room.

"I thought you were going on to Pangboche," I say.

"Look, my ankle is hurting," he says defensively. "Rather take it easy today and have a better day tomorrow."

Outside the lodge, Chumba Sherpa stands waiting, hands in his pockets, fly undone, wearing oversized women's sunglasses and a sun hat. He bounces up and down with manic energy as if carrying sixty kilos down from Gorak Shep was nothing. You could send this young man up to the top of Everest without much problem.

"I need another porter," I tell him. "I'll pay you one thousand rupees."

He laughs, knowing I'm teasing him. He shakes his head. He has a job already. I feel sorry I won't be bumping into him any more and getting the extra service he provided by acting as an ad hoc waiter.

Kumar and I continue on our way. The wind blasting down the valley behind us is cold, despite the sun. We pass three well-dressed young Sherpa men. I acknowledge them with a "*Namaste*." Pronounced Na-ma-stay, I've always liked the meaning, something like, "I salute the God within you."

"Hi," one replies with a perfectly cultivated American accent.

We cross the river and climb over the hill, then down towards Pangboche. Instead of taking the lower path we had come up, I follow Kumar on a path that leads higher, past a *mani* wall. I've come to trust Kumar, and even if the communication between us is minimal, he seems to understand intuitively so much of what I want and need. He rarely lets me get too far behind, or too far ahead, yet he provides me with sufficient space to have the sensation that I am alone on this walk, which is what I wanted.

Lost in my thoughts, I see Kevin sitting on a boulder by the path, looking at me. I stop, frozen in my tracks. But when I look again, there is no one there. It's a strange feeling. For some time after his death, I kept seeing him everywhere. Inevitably, it was someone else who looked vaguely like him. But this is the first time I've seen him, and there was no one there at all.

I am certain I saw him, hunched down, looking over his shoulder at me.

Absolutely certain.

Now I know that he's with me on this journey.

Still mystified, and a bit shaken by the apparition, I continue along the path with its beautiful view down the valley towards Tengboche, and beyond towards the hill overlooking Namche. It is a reminder how short the distances really are. Pushing it, I could be in Namche tonight, doing in one day what it had taken me eight days to do on the way up. The thought isn't so impossible under a sky clear of clouds and mountain peaks plainly visible. What a difference it makes when it's sunny. Looking down at the river far below I see a deer at the water's edge. It's a musk deer; I can see its teeth, or tusks, protruding from its upper jaw.

Unlike Lower Pangboche, which had disappointed me with its gauntlet of lodges, Upper Pangboche is an authentic Sherpa village with dwellings clustered around its *gompa,* built around 1667, and the oldest in the Khumbu. *Boche* means "field". And Pangboche means big fields. Tengboche, Dingboche, Lobuche, are all areas with large fields traditionally used for growing hay and grazing yaks during the summer months. Now they are all major stopping off points for trekkers walking up to Everest Base Camp, Everest, or other peaks.

"Kumar, you are my guide as well as my porter," I tell him. "You could charge a lot more if you worked as a guide-porter and not just as a porter. You've worked all over the Khumbu, and even if you are not a Sherpa, and do not come from here, you know all the lodges and routes. You've even walked around the Annapurna Circuit. All you need to do to work as a guide-porter is to speak English. Today I refuse to speak Nepali to you, and you are my guide. Okay? I want to go to Gokyo, and I am going to rely on you to get me there."

I no longer bother to refer to Jamie's guidebook and leave my itinerary entirely to Kumar.

He smiles shyly at this suggestion but every time he tries to say something to me in Nepali, I refuse to answer him. I follow him through a mature stand of pine trees into the village. Passing several homes that have been turned into lodges, we circumnavigate the village *gompa* where he leads me into a dark kitchen of a large building. Despite the gloom, I can see the grime-streaked face of the cook when he greets me. Kumar escorts me upstairs.

Rather than a purpose-built lodge, this is a home that has been converted into a lodge. The extra accommodation for trekkers is built around a live pine tree and the stairway has been cut out of a huge boulder. The floor above differs from the rest of the old dwelling. Plywood sheets and large glass pane windows provide a solarium-bright corner room. Despite the frigid temperatures outside, the room is warm, heated by the sun's rays all day. Kumar sees the look of satisfaction on my face and smiles.

I close the door behind him and strip off my thermal undershirt, shirt, and fleece jacket. I can smell the stale sweat. I count the days since I last had a shower, in Deboche, a week ago. I hang my sweat-stained clothes on string draped across the room. Puffs of dust float into the sunlight when I undo my bootlaces. My socks reek. I open the door to the room, place my boots and socks in the corridor and then close the door again. I collapse on the bed, my naked feet resting on the bedside table so the sunlight beaming through the windows can dry them too. It feels good to have the sunlight warm my body. I rest my head on a pillow and study my feet. The toenails are black with dirt, and crusts of black grime have collected between the toes. Blisters have formed on two toes although I had not noticed them while walking.

It feels incredibly decadent to lie back without a shirt on and bask in the warmth of the sun. Outside the window, prayer flags flap in the breeze. Behind them, providing a dramatic backdrop, is Thamserku. Through the other window, a Sherpa man stands by the stone wall of the courtyard. Judging from his stance, his contorted face and the saliva dripping down his chin, he is mentally handicapped. He stares at me through the window as I gaze back. He must wonder what I am doing semi-naked when it is so cold outside that puffs of mist are expelled from his mouth. He watches me with interest and seeing me taking note of him, he points at his mouth. His fingers are black with grime and his fingernails long and curving.

Kumar knocks on the door. I ask him to give a bundle of rupees to the man outside. He smiles when he comprehends what I want him to do. Kumar goes outside and gives the beggar the money. The crazy man looks vaguely at the bank notes. He doesn't know how to count money, although he clearly understands that it can buy him food and other things. He stuffs the money into the folds of his jacket, so impregnated with grime that the Nike logo, that international symbol of affluence and style, is almost invisible. Happy, he wobbles off down the path, his clump of tatty black hair sticking up in all directions while I lie back on the bed and close my eyes and luxuriate in the heat of the sunlight.

There is another knock on the door and I tell whomever it is, to come in.

An old lama wearing ochre robes opens the door. He carries a cup of steaming tea and laughs when he sees me lying on the bed, naked to the waist, and with bare feet. When he laughs, it's a Santa Claus kind of laugh, a deep belly laugh, but more sincere. He has a kindly, knowledgeable face, and like so many of these old lamas, exudes compassion. I swing my feet off the bedside table and he places the tea there for me.

"Thank you," I tell him, self-conscious now as I sit up. "Thanks very much." I have questions I want to ask him. Does he board here too? Is he another guest in this lodge? Why did he bring me a cup of tea? Does he see my need for spiritual enlightenment? Will he be my lama?

As if reading my mind, he laughs a deep belly laugh and backs out of the room and closes the door. If being served tea unexpectedly by a venerable lama isn't a good omen, I don't know what is. I pick up the cup of tea, and lie on my back again, head propped on a straw-filled pillow as I stare at the Himalayas outside. I am absolutely, utterly, perfectly happy. I sip the tea and reflect on what this auspicious meeting may mean. The feeling of anticipation is akin to being a kid, lying in bed on Christmas Eve, and wondering what Santa is going to bring.

The sun dips behind the mountains to the east and within minutes the room becomes cold. I stand up to put on dry clothes and gaze at the wall of mist invading the valley. I close the flimsy curtains to provide some measure of insulation against the cold during the night. In my backpack, I have several laminated photos of the Dalai Lama. I select two and walk down the stone staircase carved out of the boulder, and around the tree trunk. Inside the attached old home, behind heavy insulated curtains, is a huge dining room with a space heater in the middle and a row of benches on the outside wall. The old lama sits on a Tibetan carpet on the bench seat, surrounded by all the paraphernalia lamas have in a *gompa.* In fact, his corner of the dining room looks like a miniature *gompa.* The peacock feathers, bells, cymbals and ritual bowls full of rice and other offerings are backed with glass cabinets containing the lodge's whiskey, canned and bottled beer, toilet paper, Pringles, playing cards, chocolate. A huge Tuborg beer poster provides a backdrop. The ad reads:

Kaji Sherpa will climb Mount Everest in a world record eighteen hours.

Why is the lama sitting here? Is he a visiting lama and there is no room at the *gompa?* Who is the woman sitting in front of him? I greet them, and say something in English, but it is apparent neither can understand, or else are not willing to reply, despite the lama's earlier hospitality. I hand him the two laminated photos of the Dalai Lama. He studies them carefully and then touches the top of his skull with both photos. He shows the woman, and then carefully props one beside the paraphernalia pertaining to his role as lama, and the other he places inside his robes. He reaches for a cup sitting on the table in front of him, pours me a cup of tea with milk, and offers it to me.

I watch as he mumbles prayers read from a prayer book, carefully turning the pages over with one hand as he holds his other hand to his head. The woman talks to him, non-stop. He doesn't really seem to listen to her, and she doesn't really seem to care if he is listening. He gently rocks backwards and forwards. While he has a sweet face, full of kindness and compassion, hers is shrewd, even hard. I wouldn't want to get on the wrong side of her. Both of them must be in their sixties.

A girl, perhaps eighteen, comes into the dining room.

'Where did you get your tea?' she demands.

"He gave it to me," I reply, a bit defensive, indicating the lama sitting at the end of the bench, his eyes half closed. The old shrew barks something at the girl, but I can't understand her words.

"He gave you his own tea, and his own milk," the girl tells me. "It is real milk, from the cow outside, not powdered milk." I look out the window into the courtyard. A huge cow, or a cross between a cow and a yak, stands there. I almost feel I should apologise.

"Is this your lodge?" I ask, dodging the issue of the tea.

"Yes, my name is Tashi." That is also the name of the lodge. "I am twenty. My parents gave it to me when I was young." She looks at the lama and the old woman. "Those are my parents."

Her parents are old enough to be her grandparents. Young Tashi has a vaguely sullen, spoilt and arrogant way about her. She wears sneakers, a fashionable baseball jacket, and a baseball cap. The lama gets up and goes outside, no doubt to avoid the berating his wife is giving him for giving away his personal tea and milk. Through the window, I see him walk through the courtyard. He throws a rock at an intruding *zopkio* coming into their yard, then unlocks the door to the drop toilet and closes it behind him.

The mist has closed in the valley, obliterating the rest of the village. Occasionally a mountain summit rises out of the enveloping mist. Dark and misty down here, a discombobulated golden peak floats high above.

"Have you finished school?" I ask Tashi. She looks young enough to be fifteen.

"Yes, this year," she says. "I was at an English boarding school in Kathmandu. We had lots of freedom and I have many friends, not just Sherpa people but Gurungs, Rais, Chetris, Brahmins. Here I only have Sherpa friends." Despite her apparent distain for me, she wants to talk. "I miss school, and Kathmandu. In your country, is easy to find jobs if I learn computers? I have many Sherpa friends in America. They say they are only visiting, but then they stay illegally and work."

She asks me how she can come to America but, realising I am not American, and do not live in America, she dismisses me and turns to talks to her mother. Soon the two become embroiled in a long harangue. The words "toilet paper" keep recurring. Even the cook is hauled in from the kitchen and into the discussion.

It is too dark in the room to read, and there is no one else to talk to. I write notes, and wait. The old lama returns and takes his place again on the bench seat. During a brief lull in the heated conversation, I ask Tashi what they are talking about.

'Two trekkers bought toilet paper but we cannot remember if they paid seventy rupees for it," she says. "The cook says they did, but we don't know." And again, the embroiled controversy starts up, before Tashi leaves the room in a huff. Her mother talks incessantly at her husband, the lama, who keeps praying, chanting audibly. Tired of this interminable debate over whether the two previous trekkers did or did not pay for toilet paper, I go into the kitchen where the cook pulls out a stool for me to sit on. He puts yak dung in the fire. For the first time in the Khumbu, I notice a back-boiler system. A barrel of water at the back of the stove has pipes leading into the interior of the stove to heat the water while food is being cooked.

The cook is gregarious and happy, unlike Tashi. His name is Angani Sherpa and he is from further down the valley. He has worked at this lodge for fifteen years, before the addition was added to the original building to make it into a lodge.

"It belongs to Tashi?" I ask.

"To lama and wife." He indicates the two sitting in the dining room. "They also renting out lodge in Lobuche for three hundred thousand rupees, and big lodge in Lower Pangboche is owned by son."

The initial impression I had of the lama changes. I thought I might be in for a spiritual revelation. Instead, like it or not, I'm once again reminded of the commercialisation of the Sherpas in the Khumbu. Everyone is out to make a buck. But who can blame them?

I learn that the owner of this lodge is also the lama for the village gompa and apparently a very big lama, even bigger than the lama in Tengboche. Or so the cook tells me. I had been told in Namche that the lama of the Pangboche *gompa* was the most highly educated lama in the Khumbu, that he had the lama equivalent of a Ph.D.

"Which country?" the cook asks, giving me a close assessment.

"Bermuda."

"Berrmuda?"

"Yes. Bermuda. It is a small country, with only sixty thousand people. It's an island in the middle of the Atlantic Ocean. New York city is the closest place." North Carolina is closer but he is more likely to know New York. "Shall I find you a postcard of my country?"

My sister in Bermuda had hidden a postcard with a message written on the back. I had hoped she would come with me on this pilgrimage of sorts, but with two children it wasn't so easy for her to get away. I go up to my room and put on my fleece jacket and find the postcard. I hand it to the cook, a photo of footprints in a pink beach with an expanse of turquoise sea and blue sky. He takes the photo and holds it sideways one way, and then the other. He can't quite make out what it is. The flat horizon between sea and sky has him fooled. I have to point out the sky, the sea, and the beach with the footprints in it. Without any mountains as a reference point, the image is hard for him to comprehend and so the perspective in the photo is totally meaningless.

Tashi enters the kitchen.

"He has been away today and none of us have eaten so we are very hungry," she tells me. "He is making our dinner before yours," she adds accusingly.

I watch Angani make their dinner. His hands are black with grime, as is his face. I dread to think when he last had a thorough wash. The only reason we don't get sicker up here is because it is so cold that most of the bacteria can't survive. While Angani prepares dinner, he tells me the social gossip.

"Tashi is married to boy from owners of big lodge in Pheriche," he says.

"An arranged marriage?" I ask.

He nods. She's probably married to one of the Sherpa boys with a ponytail I had seen lounging on a sofa in the lodge I was visiting. That would be a good financial match for both families. They are both wealthy; one is the most experienced lama in the area while the other has businesses in Kathmandu. What a perfect combination, mixing the commercial elite with the spiritual elite.

"She just finishing school but now is married so no chance for going to America." He laughs. "She also has American friend, but now no is possible for marriage in America."

"She likes her husband?" I ask.

"Yes. He is very nice. But she wanting to go America too."

He laughs again at her predicament. When he has finished making their dinner, he makes me a vegetable pizza, which is nothing more than Tibetan bread with lots of chopped vegetables piled on top, coated with *nak* cheese and placed on top of the stove with a pot lid over it to make the cheese melt. Not exactly pizza, but nutritious anyway.

It's been a long walk from Gorak Shep. I say goodnight to Angani, and to Kumar who has been listening to our conversation. I head upstairs to bed, borrowing a flashlight. I perform my nightly ritual, laying out two empty water bottles beside the bed alongside my flip-flops, toilet paper for blowing my nose, the remaining cough syrup, and bottle of drinking water. When I have put everything in its place, I slip into my sleeping bag and squeeze the wax earplugs into my ears. In no time, I'm asleep.

16

Pangboche-Thare
Up the Gokyo Valley

During the night, I dreamt I was back in our home in Toronto, Canada where the family was based for some years. It was the last summer we had in that house. When my father wrote two best selling books earlier that year my parents, and then my two sisters, moved to Bermuda. Kevin and I stayed in our parent's home before it was sold. It was probably one of the times I felt closest to Kevin, just the two of us together without the interference of sisters or parents. He was running two businesses and was night manager of a Howard Johnson's, while I was working as an economist in the head office of one of Canada's largest banks. I knew I was leaving for Tanzania with the United Nations at the end of the summer and Kevin had plans to follow the rest of the family down to Bermuda. But in my dream Kevin and I were still in our family home in Toronto and I could hear Kevin's voice calling out to me, but I couldn't see him or find him. In my dream I looked in cupboards, behind closed doors, under beds, but he was nowhere, and yet I could hear him calling clearly.

Half awake, I lay in bed, the images and details of our family house so vivid, the sound of my brother's voice haunting my thoughts. I stay in my warm sleeping bag and savour the sensation of being in that house again, of being close to Kevin. Even if I couldn't see him, I could hear his voice, feel his presence. Why was he calling me? When dawn breaks outside my window, I rise and stumble down the stairs, and into the dark kitchen. Kevin and the dream follow me, wrapping me in their aura.

In the kitchen, the cook is busy washing the family's clothes.

'*Namaste*,' he greets me. And the ghost of my brother fades from my consciousness as I reluctantly re-enter this Himalayan world.

Angani's wrinkled hands are relatively clean as he takes them out of the dirty brown water and dries them on a dishcloth. He makes me a *nak* cheese omelette as we discuss Tashi again.

"Tashi wants to see friend in America," he says, "but if going America, maybe never coming back." He laughs at the notion. "Then husband is unhappy."

"And you?" I look at him. "You will work here forever?"

"Maybe next year I start work as cook for trekking company," he replies.

Several local women enter the lodge at the back entrance and disappear into the dining room. It seems as if some kind of *puja*, religious offering or prayer, is going on in there. I hear the clanging of cymbals and smell the incense. The dining room serves as an alternative prayer room, which is a lot more convenient for the lama than the cold *gompa*.

When someone in Namche told me that the lama here was very wealthy, I had asked if the charge levied on tourists who wanted to see the yeti skull in the *gompa*, before it had been stolen, had provided him with a substantial income. I was told emphatically that any money collected to see the yeti would have gone only to the *gompa* and the lama definitely would never have taken any of it. But for services like *pujas*, the lama would legitimately keep the money offered. For services such as funerals, the payment to attending lamas can be considerable.

When Kumar has helped me pack, I ask the cook for my bill.

"Tashi collects money," he says, refusing to touch the cash. Before he goes to get her, he hands me a cup of tea and says, "I give you. No charge."

Tashi comes back and goes through my bill, minus the cup of tea.

"How many pieces of *nak* cheese you have in omelette?" she demands. "Two pieces or three?"

"How would I know?" I answer. "I didn't cook it."

"One egg omelette, or two?" she persists.

"Ask the cook," I reply, testily. As an ex-lama had said to me seven years ago in Braga, on the Annapurna Circuit, "There are three religions in Nepal. Hinduism, Buddhism, and Tourism." I can hardly blame Tashi for her avarice when it's as difficult as getting blood out of a stone to persuade some trekkers to open their purse strings.

And now, of course, there is a fourth religion, the Maoism that seems to have wreaked havoc on all the other religions.

As soon as I hit the trail, the negativity of Tashi and her painstaking inspection of my bill is quickly gone. The sun is bright and warm, the sky clear of clouds and the valley devoid of mist. Far below, the turquoise river shimmers silver in the sunlight, the flashing waters rumbling audibly over rocks and boulders the size of a house. Above, the mountains are so high it does not seem possible anything so colossal could exist. No previous experience could prepare one for the gargantuan scale of the mountains here in the Khumbu.

Over the roar of the river, I hear a goat, then several more goats, bleating. Looking down the steep hillsides, which are precipitous enough to give me vertigo, I see a large Himalayan thar standing on a spur of rock. Somewhere below him must be his harem of females and their crying kids. The size of the thar is almost that of a small pony. His long brown hair and yak-like overdeveloped shoulders give him an air of menace.

Sherap at the Panorama Lodge in Namche, told me that the thar are becoming a problem. There are so many of them now that they create erosion and often eat crops painstakingly planted by the Sherpa people. Not two hundred metres further along the path, I hear and then see another herd of thar. This time I can see the females and the kids as well. There must be at least twenty thar foraging on the sheer cliffs overhanging the river.

Across the valley is the backlit Tengboche *gompa*, its roof glinting in the sunlight, towered over by the shadowy backdrop of Thamserku. From this distance, and without all the construction visible on the other side, it looks impressive, sitting on the sunny ridge overseeing the junction of the Gokyo and Imja Khola valleys. Stretches of the path are carved out of the rock. In other steep sections, the trail is built up with masonry over vertical clefts in the rock face. A momentary lack of concentration and one would easily step out into the void, and a long drop to the valley bottom.

At a small waterfall crossing the path, I notice another musk deer. He's so close I can see the tusk-like teeth, protruding over its bottom lip. Like the thar, he seems totally unconcerned by my presence, further proof of how poaching of animals has been drastically curtailed. The path turns north, towards Gokyo. Immediately below is the village of Phortse, ideally located on the comparatively flat spur of land between the two valleys. With terraced fields of buckwheat and potatoes, this village was, until the advent of tourism, the last inhabited village up either valley. Facing south so that winter sun from early morning to late afternoon bathes Phortse in sunlight, it is an ideal location. Phortse is surrounded and protected by steep cliffs below, and high mountains towering above and behind. This is the first authentic village I have seen since Khunde or Khumjung. Historically, the other settlements further up were inhabited during the summers, but abandoned during the winters. It's a warm, friendly landscape here, quite different from the desolate settlements of lodges up the valley.

Looking north into the straight Gokyo gorge I can see much further than I could up the winding valley towards Everest. As a result, the views here are more extensive and impressive. The pathways carved out of the hillsides on either side of this valley are high up its flanks, creating an entirely different perspective than the route towards Everest Base Camp, which had been for the most part, along the valley bottom. Immediately opposite Phortse, on the other side, I can see the trail, which I will descend in some days from Gokyo back to Namche. It drops abruptly down to the river before climbing along a steep ridge.

Before coming here, I imagined the Gokyo Valley as some hidden, secret valley that would be difficult to climb and very remote. I pictured it being dark and scary, a place few people went. But on this dazzling day, the impression is very different and I look forward to strolling up this beautiful glacier-gauged gorge with its incredible views. The fact that I've seen no other trekkers today is a good sign too. I was the only trekker in my lodge last night, and the only trekker in upper Pangboche as far as I could tell. Now I have walked some hours and have not seen another foreign trekker, or anyone for that matter; just two yak blocking the trail ahead of us. Kumar had to chase the recalcitrant pair off by waving his stick.

Walking below a brightly painted new *gompa* overlooking Phortse village, I follow Kumar alongside the upper stone walls of the village into dense forest, trees that were protected long ago by an edict from an environmentally aware lama. With a cool breeze and a hot sun, the weather couldn't be finer. My persistent altitude headache has gone and I am no longer out of breath walking. A diverted stream of water propels the creaking wooden blades of a revolving prayer wheel enclosed in a whitewashed stone structure. The perpetually spinning turbine-powered prayer wheel invokes the gods with minimum effort and the rhythmic squeaking of the rotating wooden barrel is as soothing a sound as the chanting of a lama.

Twice I come across Danphe, the Impeyan pheasant, with its iridescent plumage. Both times the birds do not seem concerned at my presence. I am close enough to take photos, even with my twenty-millimetre wide-angle lens.

Not far after Phortse the path hugs the steep-sided mountain with precipitous drops to the river, some four or five hundred metres below. I have learned, when I can hear the roar of the river, not to look down. The path is narrow and where it's protected from the sun's melting rays, it is icy and covered in snow, with an outward slant. One slip would mean a long vertical fall. Without crampons to steady my feet on the ice, it's frightening and I am thankful Kumar has my heavy backpack.

At Konar we enter a picturesque sheltered side valley and fields dotted with several huts. All of them are padlocked and there is no one here. At a spur jutting out of the rock face, I climb to a small peak marked with prayer flags and cairns projecting far out into the gorge. I'm afforded the most spectacular far-reaching views up and down the valley. The paths to Gokyo, etched into rock faces either side of the gorge, are visible for some distance. My stomach turns while sitting on top of the rock pinnacle, as I try to ignore the precipitous drop down to the river.

By the time we reach a small stone hut on a corner of the path we still have not seen anyone, although on the other side of the canyon I can glimpse several groups of trekkers marching like ants up to Gokyo or down to Namche. This crude mud and stone hut resembling another empty yak herder's hut is, in fact, a teahouse. Plastic sheeting on the otherwise open windows provides a measure of protection from the wind. Here, there are no cigarettes, beer, Snickers Bars, biscuits, or toilet paper. Apart from a bottle of concentrated lemon juice to make hot lemon, the only thing on offer are potatoes, boiled or fried. Kumar orders a heaping plate full of steaming potatoes and I ask for mine to be fried. The woman who prepares the food, and who lives in this freezing hut, comes from Phortse. The dark interior of the hut is basic, with dirt floor, a bed against one wall, some shelves, and a clay fireplace. She appears to be in her sixties but could be much younger. She shows Kumar and I a photograph of herself standing between two trekkers, taken when she was much younger. She admires the image of her unlined face and toothy smile. Her teeth are missing now, and her face is creased with numerous deep wrinkles. I ask if I can take her photograph and she shakes her head politely. It's a shame, since her lined face is so photogenic but she obviously thinks herself too old and unattractive.

When Kumar peels the boiled potatoes I tell him that he is not eating the most nutritious part of the potato, the skin, full of vitamins. He shrugs. To prove my point, I eat his peelings. By the time we have finished our break and re-emerge from the hut into the brightness outside, the first tendrils of evening mist float by. If I contemplate the spooky strands of clouds long enough, they resemble ghosts. I continue walking, deliberately ignoring the haunting phantoms. The ethereal images, combined with my imagination, are too ominous to brood over too long. Within half an hour, the initial curl of mist has congealed into an impenetrable bank of cloud. I regret stopping at the hut for lunch. If we had continued, we would have had another hour of unobstructed views before being socked in by the weather. As the banks of cloud build up above us, the world becomes darker and more foreboding. If anything could be likened to the afterlife, this is how I imagine it to be.

Through the mist sweeping up the mountainsides I hear, and then see several Tibetan snowcocks. They are visible for only seconds during their noisy descending flight before they disappear into the dense vapour. The screeching clucking noise they emit gliding downhill is quite different from the sounds they make while strutting like overstuffed pigeons around lodges.

Walking through the thick fog, I feel as if I am going somewhere, but I'm not really sure where. It's a strange feeling walking blindly and wilfully deeper and deeper into this murkiness. At Thore, we find one basic hut, which looks as if it might serve as a teahouse, but it too is locked. Kumar leads me through to Thare, another collection of yak herder huts twenty minutes further along the path. It's dark and cold and with the increasing gloom, I'd be grateful to find any place as shelter for the night. Through the thickening bank of cloud, I can vaguely see terraced fields ahead of us surrounded by stone walls and several slate-roofed shelters. This is yet another mountain hamlet used by villagers in the summer for grazing their yaks.

One stone building has smoke coming out of the chimney. Inside, Nima, a Sherpa girl huddles with her younger brother, Sona, in a simple hut divided into two rooms by a flimsy partition. One communal dormitory bed occupies one side of the hut and in the other are an earth stove, a bed, and a bench seat. Although not quite as rudimentary as the hut we stopped in earlier, this one provides the bare minimum for survival.

Nima asks us what we want. When we request potatoes, she puts on a jacket and ambles to the adjacent terraced field, kneels on the ground, and begins digging into a mound of dirt. She removes enough dirt to reveal a cache of potatoes buried in the earth. While Nima digs out our dinner, Sona collects water from a stream.

Knowing I will now spend some fourteen hours or more inside the smoky hut, I change into warm dry clothes and then stand outside for the fresh air. My persistence in staying outdoors despite the bone-numbing cold is rewarded with a view through a gap in the mist. Although it is dark in the valley, Cho Oyu's massive head and shoulders loom above, bathed in warm golden light. But then the peak evaporates with the mist and then the sun disappears and it becomes intensely cold, too chilly to continue standing around outside. With no mountain peaks to distract me I enter the smoky lodge and sit with the others around the yak dung fire.

Nima wears running shoes, fashionable jeans and a cheap, probably Made-in-China fleece jacket with teddy bear motives all over it. Both Nima and Sona have the classic handsome features of the Sherpa; she looks about eighteen, he about fifteen. There is obviously a good rapport between the two of them. The brother is constantly whistling or singing. We sit in front of the fire staring at the flames flickering through the opening in the mud oven. The brother and sister don't speak English, and my Nepali is not sufficient to have a sustained conversation.

While she cooks, he fetches the water and firewood. On the windowsill, two jars full of kerosene with burning wicks serve as light. It's so quiet it's downright eerie. Besides the hissing of the pressure cooker, and the crackling of the logs burning in the fire, there are no other sounds.

17

Thare-Gokyo
The Gokyo Lakes

During the night, a rhythmic creaking woke me. At first I thought it must be someone fanning the fire. I lifted my head to see if it was Kumar, but his form, beside me on the platform bed, was inert under several blankets. He was sound asleep. The repetitive noise continued for some time. It sounded very much like the creaking of a bed when a couple makes love. There was a sigh, as if someone has had had an orgasm, and then silence.

Confused, I drifted back to sleep.

This morning, Nima is awake early, feeding the fire. Her brother sleeps in. They have both slept in the same bed. Surely they are not lovers, but as if to confirm this indeed might be the case, she tenderly hands him a cup of hot tea as he lies under the covers.

Outside, mist completely obscures the valley. I walk a hundred metres along the path and then climb a little higher. I quietly squat, my back facing the void. Concentrating for several minutes on my efforts, I look up, startled by the sudden apparition of what appears to be a yeti. It's a large male thar, facing me, much closer than the ones I saw the day before. With his massive shaggy brown mane over his shoulders, his front end large and formidable, he seems to be standing on two legs and the resemblance to a hairy, broad-shouldered yeti is obvious. He turns sideways, confirming he really is a thar, and saunters off, unconcerned as I bury my business under a couple of rocks.

The only other person residing in the collection of half a dozen shelters is an old yak herder. I study him while brushing my teeth. His role seems to entail getting up, walking out the door of his stone shelter, tossing a few well-aimed stones at eight yak to get them moving up the hillside, leaving them all day to feed, and then herding them back into the enclosure in the evening.

By the time Kumar and I set off, mist still clogs the valley. The path is slippery where the water has frozen solid overnight. There is an increasing sense that winter is moving in. One day soon there will be a heavy snowstorm and access to the valley will be completely cut off. I wouldn't want to have to walk back out along this slippery, steep path after deep snowfall.

Huge boulders inscribed with Tibetan Buddhist prayers precede the path's gradual descent to the river at Na, where a couple of lodges sit huddled by the stream. We cross a wooden bridge covered in frozen spray and then climbing up the other side, I see smoke. Is it a body being cremated by the river? I ask Kumar and point at the smoke.

"*Puja?*" I ask hopefully. I still have my own envelope to burn. He shakes his head.

"Porters eating lunch."

On the other side of the valley we join the more frequently used track leading directly from Namche to Gokyo. Acclimatised after my walk up to Gorak Shep and Kala Pattar, the stroll up here, although over four and a half thousand metres high, is no longer the effort it was when I ascended the Everest Valley. As the mist clogging the gorge disappears in the heat of the sun, on a flat piece of grassy ground clear of snow, I see two trekkers lying on the grass, sunning themselves. I recognise the Grumpy Couple.

"Are you the two who fired your porter in Lobuche without paying him for the day's work?" I ask, very innocently.

I'm sure they remember me. I was the only other trekker who had witnessed the whole thing. He sits up, leaning on his elbows.

"Yes?" he says, with a slightly aggressive tone.

"The police are looking for you in Tengboche and Namche."

I carry on walking before they see the smile creasing my face. That will teach them to be so inconsiderate of their porter.

Kumar waits for me, sitting ahead on the path, eating a packet of Rara noodles raw, as if they were potato chips. He carries packets of noodles with him, and when he knows a lodge owner or the cook, he uses their boiled water and his own noodles rather than eat the more expensive meals at the lodge. The path is covered in a sheet of slippery ice where it's cut into a rock face overhanging the Dudh Kosi. I traverse a barely visible ice-covered wooden bridge made from a couple of hefty tree trunks and ascend over the lip of a crest. I have suddenly accessed a hidden valley. The shimmering blue lake in front of me is totally unexpected, although this is of course, Gokyo Lakes. A woman with a huge backpack stands motionless by the snow-covered path, staring at ducks sitting on the thin layer of ice covering the pond.

"Those ducks are frozen in the ice," she says with a distinct Aussie accent.

The ducks aren't frozen, they're sleeping, their heads turned around, their beaks nestled under their wings for warmth. To the right, on the far side of the pond are several more brown ducks feeding off the bottom, their tails in the air.

"Looks like some have frozen upside down," I tell her.

"Ah, yeah," she replies, not sure if I'm being serious or not.

Leaving her to ponder the fate of the ducks, I reach a second, larger lake, turquoise-coloured rather than deep blue and enveloped on three sides by steep-sided mountains. On the fourth side is the lateral moraine of the Ngozumpa Glacier. The view is magical, the bright gay colour of the lake a welcome change from the desolate browns, greys, blacks and whites of the valley and mountains. A metre or so of snow lies on the ground all around. This lake too has a thin layer of ice covering half of it. Tiny wavelets blow across the lake trapping air under the ice, which makes a strange, almost electronic sound. Occasionally there's a loud crack as the ice cleaves. At the top end of the lake, in the small icy stream feeding it, I see a small reddish-brown dipper fly onto a rock and then dive into the water, disappearing from sight.

Walking along the boulder-cluttered path covered in snow, I come to yet another larger and even more beautiful lake, also surrounded on three sides by steep mountains and the ridge of lateral moraine. Ahead of me, easily visible, is the hill of Gokyo Ri, similar in size and overall height to Kala Pattar. Below, on one side of the lake, is an assortment of lodges. A sign indicates that the *Gokyo Resort* lodge, reputed to be the best, is higher up and overlooking the others. None of these ramshackle stone buildings look remotely like a resort, but I like the optimism. I walk with determination past the Gokyo Resort's tuck store full of chocolate goodies and a "library" comprising of several shelves of new and used books. Half a dozen trekkers sit facing the lake and the amphitheatre of mountains, soaking up the warm rays of the sun. It could be a ski resort. Tracks, probably left by snowboards, curve in long S parallels through the snow.

A pretty blonde-haired woman, English, sits in the middle of five men who form a semi-circle around her. I recognise members of the British Army group sitting huddled together in another corner. And in the courtyard of the lodge down below, washing his face in a bowl of hot water, the Lufthansa doctor/pilot. The loquacious Talkative Climber is here too, still wearing his gaiters and scarf wrapped over his head pirate fashion. Just as before, he recounts to everyone who will listen, particularly the pretty blonde, all the details of his trip over the Cho La pass. At least The Accountant isn't here, with his snorts and unending advice. Sherpa guides and porters sit inside the solarium playing cards while one of them strums a guitar. Kumar asks me for another advance and then, within minutes, is gambling with the others.

"You want a room?" a slightly rotund Nepalese man wearing a baseball cap and Ray Ban aviator sunglasses asks. He reminds me of Yogi Bear, with his portly stomach and trousers hoisted tight around his belly.

"You're the owner?" I ask, astonished. He doesn't look like a Sherpa from the Khumbu.

"This is my lodge, with my wife," he replies.

"You look more like a Brahmin than a Sherpa," I say candidly.

"You are right," he says, and laughs. "I am from Biratnagar, in the Terai." Nothing could be less likely than to find such a man here. The Terai is the flat stretch of Nepal bordering India and Bangladesh, not much higher than sea level. Yet here he is, running one of the highest altitude lodges in the country. But more importantly, Brahmins generally consider themselves well above Sherpas in the traditional caste system. In fact, Sherpas are "untouchables", while Brahmins are at the top of the pile, the priestly caste.

"How does someone from the Terai end up owning a lodge here in Gokyo?"

As he talks, he leads me to a building built on a terrace behind the solarium.

"I worked as an accountant at the Everest View Hotel where I met my wife," he says. "She is a Sherpa from Khumjung. We married and her father gave us this land to build the lodge."

We climb the steps to the upper terrace.

"There is my wife, Ranchi Sherpa."

He points at a woman brushing her shiny black hair and talking to another Sherpa woman on the sunny terrace of the lodge below.

A telephone rings and he quickly excuses himself to run into the solarium and answer it. This does not match my pre-conceived notion of what Gokyo would be like.

He returns a minute later.

"My name is Shrendra Sharma," he says, and extends his hand.

"You have telephone service here?" I ask.

"Satellite telephone service," he clarifies. "It is as expensive to phone Europe or America as Namche or Kathmandu. That was a friend from Pheriche, saying he was going back to Namche and for me to meet him there."

He shows me a room with a single double bed. He pats the bed and straightens the threadbare dirty sheet over the sponge mattress.

"Two hundred rupees," Shrendra tells me. This is twice the normal rate of a hundred rupees for a single room, but still less than three dollars. For a Nepalese, this place too must be a licence to print money.

"You've got something special on your menu you can suggest?" I ask hopefully. The usual selection of fried noodles and Tibetan bread under a variety of guises is starting to wear thin.

"How about sweet-corn soup and yak stroganoff?" he asks.

Huh? I follow him down to the main building, which comprises the dormitory, dining room and kitchen. And I had thought this would be the most desolate, remote part of the trip. It certainly isn't as frequented as much as the ascent to Kalar Pattar and Everest Base Camp but it's a much more beautiful, colourful walk. The walk up the valley has sunny views directly to the south and once over the lip, the lakes add colour and energy to these lifeless altitudes.

Instead of desolation, I find sweet-corn soup, yak stroganoff, single rooms, solariums and a telephone. Shrendra hands me a menu. I place my order and within minutes of him disappearing into the kitchen, I am served hot sweet-corn soup. When I'm finished, he serves me a plate heaped with rice and topped with yak stroganoff.

"This actually tastes like stroganoff," I tell him.

"We add our own pickled cucumber," Shrendra says, proudly. "That's what gives it the special stroganoff taste."

Unbelievable.

I vaguely listen to The Talkative Climber who hasn't stopped bragging since I arrived. He has fierce competition from the others though, including a longhaired Kiwi who has a more laid-back technique, perhaps because he also has a joint held tightly between his thumb and forefinger. He seems to impress the blonde Englishwoman with the fact that he is a ski instructor back home.

Sitting in a sheltered quiet corner, I watch hundreds of sparrows harass an eagle until it flies away. There are plenty of choughs as well, riding the currents of air. Early in the afternoon, mist forms at the lip of the valley and wafts across the lake like dry ice drifting over the stage of a theatre. At first, the strands of mist dissipate but soon they are thick enough to scoot up the slope of Gokyo Ri. I try to judge whether it's worth climbing Gokyo Ri now, or if the mist is going to envelope the hill and obstruct the view.

The commanding NCO of the British Army group recognises me.

"We're heading down tomorrow," he says. "Christina's climbing Gokyo Ri right now. She was hoping to see you."

I ask Shrendra for his advice.

"Do you think with all this mist that it's worth climbing Gokyo Ri now?"

"No problem," he tells me, as he looks at the lake. "Up at the top it will be clear and you will have a beautiful view."

I tell Kumar that I am leaving to climb Gokyo Ri, but he is too busy playing cards and dismisses me with a wave of his hand. It's just past 2 o'clock when I walk across the boulders straddling the small stream that is the start of the Dudh Kosi and begin the hill climb. The path splits immediately into dozens of different trails, the ones on the shadowy northern side leading through heavy snow.

The first group I meet coming down are the last people on the mountain.

"There's no one else up there," the Sherpa guide tells me.

I have obviously missed Christina, perhaps because of the mist. But this is what I had hoped for, to be alone. Perhaps at the top of Gokyo Ri I will find solace. Perhaps I will find that special spot where I can feel good about burning the envelope, and the last mortal remains I have of my brother. It's beginning to feel that way.

The mist blows across the lake and when it embraces me it chills me to the bone. I climb at a steady pace but now the altitude does not affect me at all. I'm surprised by how much I have acclimatised, with no headache and little shortness of breath as I push myself to climb faster. How much easier it is to walk when one doesn't have a headache. This is how most trekkers feel after only a few days of acclimatisation. For me, it has taken over two weeks and I have been doing everything right: drinking lots of water, not climbing more than three hundred metres a day, whenever possible climbing high and sleeping low.

Half way to the top, the mist suddenly thickens and wraps me in its icy grip. A dozen Tibetan snow cock run up the slope at an implausible speed, making a loud sound as they go, as if protesting over the pursuing clouds of cold and damp. The pace at which these fat birds can run uphill is impressive. The mist drifts up and down, around and about, until once again I walk out of it and can see the top of Gokyo Ri. It takes me one and a half hours, from the time I left the lodge, to reach the boulders at the summit where numerous colourful Buddhist prayer flags flutter in the wind. Climbing on the boulders, trying to avoid the ice and snow, I find a flat-topped slab of rock. Although the walk up here is comparable to Kala Pattar and not particularly steep, on the other side of the summit a glacier has carved away at the peak and the drop is sheer enough that no snow clings to the rock face.

I survey the scene. To the west, the sun sets. To the east, shadowy fingers reach for the tops of the mountains. Lhotse, its yellow band distinct in the setting sunlight, casts its long shadow over Everest behind it. A plump caterpillar-like white cloud inches its way up the valley, covering the long Ngozumapa glacier. Veins of mist break off from the main body of cloud and scoot up over the lakes. Far to the south are Ama Dablam and Thamserku, bathed in the evening light. Standing alone here at five and half thousand metres, there is a sense of what it might be like to climb a high mountain. Once again, the views below are stupendous and the feeling of being above it all must be similar, albeit on a much smaller scale, to being on the summit of Everest.

I remain transfixed by the scene. The fluttering prayer flags add their spiritual feel to the place. A lone yellow-billed chough hovers above, its wings and tail folding and twisting with the gusts of wind. He and I are the only two up here, and he eyes me carefully. This could be an auspicious sign, perhaps a spirit pulling alongside me to convey a message. Or it could just be a chough looking for signs of discarded food: a piece of chocolate, crumbs from crackers, biscuits or bread.

The sun dips behind the summit of mountains to the west and instantly it grows colder. It's frightening how cold one can get when the sun goes down. I'm not sure if this is a genuine physical sensation, or whether it is psychological as well. When the sun disappears, it feels scarily lonely up here, and I have nothing with me except the clothes I am wearing. The warmth of the sunlight is an ally, while the cold and darkness quickly becomes the enemy. When the sun sinks below the towering horizon I feel the fear, conscious of the fact that I am in an inhospitable environment. I think of those dead climbers slumped in the snow and ice, even their ghosts unable to descend the mountain they climbed. It sends shivers through me. And as much as I love these mountains, they also scare me. I reach inside my Goretex jacket and grope for the envelope. But it just doesn't seem right to burn it here, despite the magnificent views.

The sun finally sets on the summits of Lhotse and Everest and the colours change dramatically from yellow to bright orange and red as the shadows creep up the mountains. The sky above the mountains blushes pastel colours: from pink, to mauve, to steel blue and dark purple, until eventually the clouds have lost all their colour and the mountains are silver against a darkening sky. A crack, like a rifle shot, echoes as an avalanche crashes down a mountainside. Not wanting to duplicate my recent feat on Kala Pattar when I had descended in the dark, I scramble off the rocks and head down before I realise I have left my walking stick at the top. I turn and climb back up to retrieve it, more for sentimental reasons than anything else. After all, the stick had served me well all the way up and it would seem ungrateful to abandon it now. The quick scramble back up to the top is a reminder of how much easier it is to descend. My heart thumps wildly by the time I reach the stick. But I also realise how much my back has healed over the last three weeks of hard walking.

Annabel will be impressed.

With the stick back in hand, I descend as quickly as I can. Halfway down, I re-enter the bank of cloud that has slowly ascended the hill. Walking into the mist is as if several layers of gauze are covering my eyes. It becomes dank and I can smell yak dung. The views of the mountains are ghostly, until they disappear altogether. But when the mist mysteriously dissipates, the black and silver mountains are suddenly apparent again for a few precious moments before the mist drifts across them like a veil.

The trail is easier to follow. Although it's getting dark, I can hear waves lapping from the lake somewhere below, as they slap against the pebbled shore. Soon, in the distance through the mist, I see the lights from the lodge shining at me like friendly beacons.

Back in my frigid room I undress and stand still for a few minutes, arms raised, so that my overheated body can cool down. My shirt, which I hang on a hook behind the door, steams, as does my body. After a few minutes in the frigid air, I dress in dry clothes and enter the dining room, full of coughing trekkers. The Talkative Climber is still talking, this time to an older man who seems to be alone. The blonde girl plays cards, surrounded by her admirers. The Lufthansa doctor, sitting beside the space heater in the centre of the room, plays the guitar, surrounded by approving Nepalese porters and guides.

Christina sits with the British Army soldiers. She extracts herself from the centre of the group and joins me at the end of a table where I have managed to find a seat.

"How was Gokyo Ri?" she asks.

"Wonderful," I tell her. I'm still on a high from the experience. "I was there by myself. The sunset was spectacular. Someone told me you were up there, but I missed you. How was it for you?"

"Good," Christina says, "but I was with a whole group so it wasn't quite as inspirational. It took us three hours to get up there. Can you imagine? This is the British Army we're talking about. I think I'm fitter than most of them. Two had to go down with altitude sickness."

I don't ask whether they dropped their drawers again at the top. I order potatoes with cheese cream sauce, and another round of sweet-corn soup and a thermos of hot lemon. When the hot lemon arrives, I pour myself a cup, and one for Christina. But as soon as I drink mine, I start coughing again.

"Did you ever think that the citrus acid in the hot lemon is aggravating your throat?" she asks.

She's right. At Kala Pattar, the same thing happened after I had had two thermoses of hot lemon. And the day before, when we stopped for lunch and I ordered a hot lemon, I had started coughing. I pass Christina the pot.

"Your throat is okay, so you're welcome to finish this," I tell her. "I'll stick to hot water from now on."

Christina pours herself another hot lemon, then turns to look at me.

"You never said what your brother Kevin died from."

The question comes out of nowhere.

"A massive heart attack," I reply,

"But he was younger than you," she says. "Was it genetic? Bad diet? No exercise? Stress?"

"Probably all of those," I answer, "but stress was probably the biggest factor. He wasn't overweight until the last four years, and even then, he wasn't overweight by much. He didn't really smoke, just on social occasions after a meal."

"You two seem so different."

"We are." I still use the present tense when I speak of my brother.

"He didn't know he was sick?"

"For the last year, he thought he had heartburn. But he refused to see a doctor. He was probably scared of what he would find out."

"I'm sorry," Christina puts her hand on my shoulder.

I think again of how Kevin organized the quadruple by-pass that saved our mother's life. He could have easily saved himself, too. He worked so hard to retire early. There were so many dreams, so many things he still wanted to do. He could have been master of his own fate. In the end he was the master of his own fate.

I remember three years earlier, when he had driven me to the airport. I was on my way back to Norway, after spending almost three months in Bermuda helping my mother recover from her quadruple by-pass. I had already checked through the airline counter and it was time for me to say goodbye. Never one to be tactile or emotional, Kevin gave me a bear hug. For the first time ever, he said to me, "I love you." And then he turned around and quickly walked away. I ran after him. "I love you too," I said. And I hugged him back.

I have carried the sadness of his death with me up into these mountains, as if it's a pack strapped to my back. Now, sitting here in this lodge, half listening to the incessant drone of the Talkative Climber, my journey is almost over. I feel the weight of emotions lightening. I can sense myself changing, just as these massive mountains are perpetually changing.

"I wish I had had one more chance to tell him, to show him, that I still loved him," I tell Christina.

And within minutes, the weight is gone.

18

Gokyo Lakes
The Conclusion

I sit up in my sleeping bag, eyes so swollen I can barely open them. The urine in the one bottle I have filled is cloudy. I am dehydrated again. The air temperature is numbingly cold. I slip out of the sleeping bag and scrape frost off a corner of the window with a fingernail. Mist blankets the view. Inside the dining room there are a few trekkers and Nepalese huddled around the space heater. The Talkative Climber wears his bright red gaiters and tells everyone about what kind of crampons are needed to cross over the Cho La. He expands on the merits of snowshoes to anyone who will listen, and then, when he exhausts that subject, he talks about the advantages of the layering system: Goretex and fleece versus down jackets.

The British Army group is leaving. I go over to their lodge. When I see Christina, I wish her a good trip back to Kathmandu and England.

"Keep in touch won't you?" I tell her. "It's been really great bumping into you."

The last time we said goodbye, in New Zealand, I never thought we'd see each other again. I was wrong then, so perhaps we'll meet yet another time. I help her load up her pack onto her back and then open the front door of her lodge. We hug each other, and then she is off.

"Take care of your back," she calls out.

"I will," I shout back as I head to my lodge. "Keep those army boys in line."

Christina laughs, and then she's gone.

The Talkative Climber and the longhaired, dope-smoking Kiwi head off for Nameless Fangs. These are the rocky outcrops just above the Fourth Gokyo Lake. They have never been formally named, but for years foreign trekkers have called them, simply, Nameless Fangs.

"How was your trip further up the valley yesterday?" I ask the Lufthansa doctor, before he departs for Namche.

"I came back at ten thirty last night," he answers.

"You must be joking," I respond.

"I went further than the sixth lake and climbed a ridge," he says. "The guidebook says it is okay to climb, but there were many rocks and it was dangerous. There is deep snow and the path is sometimes not so easy to see. I fell in the snow up to my waist when I went off the path. It was difficult."

He washes his face in a basin of hot water, covers his blonde hair with a woollen hat, wipes his eyeglasses clean, and then he's off for Namche. I decide to stay another day and walk to Nameless Fangs from the top of which, according to Jamie's book, is an even better view of Everest than from the summit of Gokyo Ri.

Despite a big breakfast of cheese and mushroom omelette with toast, I have no energy. I give Kumar the day off and he happily joins other porters, playing cards in the sunroom. With only a small backpack, I stroll lazily north towards Nameless Fangs and the fifth and sixth lakes. The temperature is at least ten degrees colder than the day before. Despite sheepskin-lined gloves, the tips of my fingers are soon frozen. The air all around is bursting with tiny ice crystals that shine like diamond dust floating in space. Hoarfrost covers wherever the sun had melted the snow on the rocky ground. Sunlight shimmers silvery off the patches of turquoise lake, and the mountains above are so white and bright with snow that I must squint, even with my sunglasses on. Although there's only half as much oxygen up here, the air is clean and uncontaminated.

I close my eyes and imagine I'm drifting with the clouds. Now that I'm acclimatized, it will take me only two days and two nights to walk back to Lukla. From there, I will climb aboard the Twin Otter with the duct tape on its wings, for the hop back to Kathmandu. From Kathmandu, it will be a flight to Qatar, then London, and then back home to Bermuda, where Annabel will meet me at the airport. We had been dating only a few months when Kevin died, and after my accident I became physically, and emotionally, dependent on her. One reason I came alone on this trip without Annabel was to regain my sense of independence. Only two months after being free of my back braces I've walked to Everest Base Camp, defying my doctors' predictions. Now, Annabel and I will have an opportunity to think about the future, maybe even talk of having our own children one day.

I pat the envelope in my breast pocket to make sure it is there. To warm both hands, I tightly clasp a plastic bottle of hot water as I negotiate the path strewn with boulders and buried in places under a metre of snow. I have so little ambition today, it's almost as if I'm sleepwalking. I climb slowly, stopping every few metres to think.

Sometimes, I lose the track and sink thigh-deep in snow. Updrafts of mist break free, skidding across the lake and up the sides of Gokyo Ri. They form shapes, sometimes with rainbow colours. I think about Kevin again, for he's still such a strong presence, as if he can see me walking here, despite the vastness of the Himalayas.

I wonder what does he think now, of his old ambitions, of the additions to his house by the beach, the publishing deals, the businesses he left behind? Does he realise that none of it was worth the struggle? That life is too short? That we must enjoy the time we have on this earth? Does he know, now, that we can't take our successes with us? Sometimes, I wonder what he thinks about Katie and Cooper, his two children. I wonder if he can remove himself from them, knowing that they, too, are masters of their own destiny, and that they, too, must pass from this world to the next. Is he liberated from all earthly things, free even from attachment to his children? Has he reached enlightenment, wherever he is, now that none of this matters?

The thought of continuing on for hours just to climb Nameless Fangs loses its appeal. I realise that I am doing what most of us do during our lifetimes. I've set myself one goal, Kala Pattar above Everest Base camp, and then the summit of Gokyo Ri. Now I'm setting myself another objective, higher and better. The views from Kala Pattar and Gokyo Ri were spectacular. Just to stand on top of those hills, at eighteen and a half thousand feet or five and a half thousand metres, and see the surrounding mountains and the glaciers and the valleys below, was worth the entire trip. But to climb another hill, to get a slightly different perspective, even if it's better, is not worth it. We do this all our lives. We pay off the mortgage of our house, but when that's done, we want to buy a bigger house in a better neighbourhood. We want to own a car; but once we own a car, we want a newer one. And in walking to Nameless Fangs, I'm doing exactly the same thing. How can another view of Everest, from a slightly different hilltop, add more to my life?

I'm not going to do that.

I'll enjoy this walk today for what it's worth. There is no destination. There is no end, no purpose; the way is the journey.

How did John Lennon put it? "Life is what happens while you're making plans."

Those first weeks after Kevin died, I was depressed. I could see no meaning to life. I even felt I understood why people committed suicide. It was because they saw beyond the succession of carrots held in front of their noses. They realized how useless it all is. But the gift of life is also beautiful, not to be abused or wasted.

How can I not be grateful for my greatest gift this year: my ability to walk despite my injuries, to undertake a trek in these magnificent mountains, through forests, along streams and lakes. Perhaps I have Kevin to thank for that. Maybe one day I'll find out.

Instead of rushing off up the valley and back before dark, I lie down on a patch of dry grass and watch the first wisps of the midday mist appear. The ethereal formations twist and turn into fantastic shapes, and then almost as quickly, disappear. Sometimes they do look like phantoms, witches, and wizards, as if the population of the netherworld had been given a day's break to play in the wind. Hundreds of yellow-billed choughs cavort in the strands of mist slithering up Gokyo Ri. The birds seem to be having fun, like kids in a playground. Sometimes, they disappear in the thickening cloud. Other times the mist evaporates and it's only the birds competing in the currents of air.

One day I would like my own ashes thrown to the winds, on a spur of rock on the high route overlooking the Manang Valley, on the Annapurna Circuit. But this is not the place for me to burn the envelope with Kevin's hair. I remember how I felt the night before, on the top of Gokyo Ri, how scary and lonely it can seem without the reassuring light and warmth of the sun. It's a cold and desolate setting in the winter, and besides, Kevin has nothing in common with the climbers who died here.

Out of the corner of my eye I see a movement. A curious weasel pokes his head out of the rocks. He has a beautiful face with tiny rounded ears. His intelligent eyes are little black buttons as they stare at me intently. His body is tan coloured and sleek. At my slightest movement he darts into the crevices under the rubble of boulders. Then he reappears moments later, at the entrance to another cleft in the rocks, each time slightly closer than the last. He's as fascinated with me as I am with him.

Tucked away like this on a patch of yak pasture in an elevated valley, surrounded by the highest mountains in the world, is a humbling experience. I lie here, savouring the day, a day that is going nowhere. I decide I won't climb another peak. Instead, I will watch, and listen, and feel, and think. This is what life should be all about. This day doing nothing, going nowhere, gives me the most.

I open my eyes and see mist trying to break over the ridge again, wafting backwards and forwards. But it does not reach me, and I am left in the warm sunlight, under a blue sky, the snow-covered ridges on either side concentrating the sun like a solar reflector. Wisps of vapour float over the crest below and drift across the turquoise lake, but they do not cover me with their cold dampness. There is no sound, not a ghostly whisper. I listen to the silence. Here in the Himalayas, far above the turmoil of the world somewhere below, my dreams actually seem real.

Lying half awake, half asleep, in a yak pasture, I know for certain that I will not burn the envelope here. To say goodbye to Kevin from the top of the world isn't what I should do. I love these mountains and they are a small part of me, but they are not where my brother belongs. It was wonderful to share this adventure and to have him with me, close to my heart. It's been a hard journey, but a necessary one. I have grown to accept Kevin's death by reliving our times together, by remembering him with all my heart.

But perhaps the envelope belongs back in the drawer in our mother's bedside table.

Perhaps I'll take the envelope on future adventures.

One day, when they are older, I will give the envelope to Katie and Cooper. Maybe they will take him on their adventures.

That would be nice.

The wind whistles through the wings of dozens of snow pigeons soaring by, descending from out of nowhere. The sun beats down, warming my face and my body, soothing me, making me sleepier.

It is so quiet I wonder if this is what Kevin feels.

Biography

Although his family has been in Bermuda for over thirty years, Andrew was born in Canada, and then spent his childhood in Hong Kong, India, Kenya, Scotland, Malaysia and Singapore. He studied postgraduate international economics in France, Canada and Norway and worked as an international economist for two Canadian banks before joining the United Nations Development Programme. He was assigned to the UNDP offices in Dar es Salaam, Tanzania, remained in the country after a two year stint with the UN, obtained his pilot's licence and started a safari company in the Selous Game Reserve. After five years in East Africa he returned to North America to become a financial advisor, and to upgrade his pilot's licence. He has subsequently worked as a consultant in international development for the Canadian, Norwegian and Swedish governments, travelling over most of Africa and Asia. He was owner of two adventure companies in Norway. He currently lives in Bermuda with his Kiwi wife Annabel and daughters Elsa and Somers where he writes and researches whales full time.

Andrew's first travelogue, *Annapurna Circuit: Himalayan Journey* was published by Constable and Robinson in 1997.

His second travelogue, *Kiwi Tracks: A New Zealand Journey* was published by Lonely Planet in its Journeys series in 1999 and rejacketed in 2005.

His travelogue on Norway, *Summer Light: A walk across Norway* was published by Lonely Planet in the spring of 2002.

Travels in Outaback Australia: Beyond the Black Stump came out January 3rd 2003 published by Travellers Eye. The Australasian edition was published in August 2003 by Allen and Unwin under the title *OUT BACK: Adventures of an Intrepid Interloper*.

Annapurna Circuit: Himalayan Journey was translated and published in German by Frederking and Thaler under the title *Rund um den Annapurna* in September 2001. A second German edition was published by National Geographic Adventure Press in July 2003.

Through their National Geographic imprint, Frederking and Thaler have also published *Trekking in Neuseeland* in November 2004,

Meine Reise Durch das Outback in October 2005, *Mittsommer: Auf Trekkingtour in Norwegen* in 2006 and *Mein weg zum Mount Everest: Auf dem Trekking* in 2007.

Andrew's photographic book on the Himalayas, *A Nepalese Journey: On foot around the Annapurnas* was published in Britain by Constable and Robinson and in India by Rupa and by The Mountaineers Books in the USA under the title *A Nepalese Journey: The essence of the Annapurna Circuit* in 2002.

Andrew's photographs and articles have featured on the front covers in international magazines including: *Royal Geographical Society Magazine*, *The Great Outdoors* (TGO), *Global Adventure*, *The Globalist*, *Action Asia*, *Destinations*, *RG*, *Bottom Line Magazine*, *Outside Australia*, British Airways in-flight magazine *High Life* and Singapore Airlines in-flight magazine *Silver Kris*.

He has completed a novel set in Namibia, South West Africa. *Skeleton Coast: The Forbidden Zone* has been translated into Japanese and published in Japan.

Since the arrival of his two daughters, Andrew has written two children's books. *The Turtle who ate a Balloon* and *The Adventures of Bermuda's Toad with One Eye*.

Andrew's first documentary film, *Paving Shangri La*, about the road being built through the Annapurna Himals, was awarded an Honorary Mention at its first showing, the Bermuda International